ec·o·nom·ics

a simple twist on normalcy

Kersten L. Kelly

Talisman Book Publishing LLC, Chicago

theeconomicsbook.com

Published by Talisman Book Publishing LLC, Chicago

ec·o·nom·ics: a simple twist on normalcy. Copyright © 2012 by Kersten L. Kelly. All rights reserved.

theeconomicsbook.com

Designed by Lauren M. Harrington

Library of Congress Catalog Number: 2011945911

ISBN-13: 978-0-578-09907-1
ISBN-10: 0-578-09907-1

Printed in the United States of America

I dedicate this book to my parents, Gene and Janice, and sister Stephanie. No matter what, they have always given me unconditional support to chase my dreams.

Contents

Preface

I've always been an ambitious person, and I strive to set attainable goals for myself. Typically, there are far too many to-do's on my plate at any given time, and I've learned to function successfully by keeping exceptionally busy. When I graduated from college, I found myself working hard in a challenging sales role for a large corporation, but my drive to further educate myself sparked my interest in post-graduate education.

Six months after graduating from college, I built my first house in a very rural area where I worked, and I did not have much to do when I came home from work at night. I had grown up in a suburb of busy Chicago, so this slower-paced community was quite an adjustment. Since I am an antsy person who can seldom sit still for very long, I decided to study for the GMAT (Graduate Management Admission Test) after taking a one-year hiatus from school. I was ready to be intellectually challenged again and longing for discussions of relevant business topics and events with my fellow peers. At the time, I hoped the outcome of that little endeavor would be a piece of paper with M-B-A written on it.

For the next year and nine months, I spent time learning the meaning of time management. I was juggling a weekly forty-hour work schedule with at least twenty to thirty hours of studying and schoolwork each week. I headed out to work in the morning, only to return home to a pile of papers, tests, and analytical problems waiting to be solved. I devoted a significant number of hours to the program. Sometimes I enjoyed "life in the fast lane," but at other times, I really was longing for some good ol' rest and relaxation.

I did my best to maintain an active social life and a positive reputation at work, as well as spending time with my family, all while earning my graduate degree. I would even venture to say that I managed this successfully. It afforded me the opportunity to do a little international traveling to The Netherlands, Belgium, Italy, Iceland, and India during the program to enhance my global knowledge and education.

Finally, I finished my last quarter of classes. When I stood among my peers at graduation, we were huddled in an atrium before we walked across the stage. Everyone was snickering about how much "free time" they were going to have when they were done, and suddenly, something about that made me quite nervous. My schedule had been so full of work, school, socializing, and family events that I could not imagine what I would do with at least twenty extra hours of free time each week. The truth is, I almost began to panic at the thought.

I considered additional educational programs and came to the conclusion that I needed to move on with life and pursue other interests. Earning an MBA was now checked off my list, and another graduate degree wasn't going to advance my career or make my life any more fulfilling than it already was. I made a decision to make a list of the activities that I had been contemplating for years and to actually do them instead of just thinking and talking about it. I decided to follow the wise and oft-used words of the poet Horace, "Carpe diem!" or "Seize the day!" This was a perfect segue into the most intense personal development chapter of my life.

I took the opportunity to use my free time to grow as a person. I started to set goals for myself, somewhat of a bucket list, assuming there was no better time than the present to start checking things off.

After contemplating what I should attempt first, I decided to become a runner. My first feat was to train myself on how to run a half-marathon. I started training, and within just four short months, I had successfully finished two races. In the process, I learned that I actually liked running, and at the time of the writing of this book, I am in the process of training for a full marathon.

My second goal was to complete a book and publish it. I've been writing stories since I was a little kid, begging my parents, friends, and sometimes classmates to read them. I want to thank my family and friends for reading all the goofy nonsense I've written over the years and for encouraging me to keep writing. This brings me to the present, for you are about to read my very first attempt at a book. I can only make one promise: This book was written with heart.

It may sound strange that a book about economics could be written with heart, but the truth is, I am extremely enlightened by the subject. I find it utterly fascinating, and it is responsible for driving all of the normal activities we do in our daily lives, though it is disguised in the form of general transactions. It is under-recognized considering its dominance and constant presence in society. The aim of this book is to provide you with a simplistic representation of what economics entails in a variety of forms, and we will use portions of well-known economic theories to explain normal activities. As you read this, my first book, I hope you will share in my passion for economics and for writing and that it will inspire you as writing inspires me...

Introduction

A Challenge to Question the Norm

There is nothing more mind-blowing than walking into the stadium that your favorite football team calls home and soaking in the atmosphere around you. As painted, foam hand-waving, excited fans pile in at a rapid rate, everything becomes almost mute in spite of the noise, and the smell of freshly cut grass encompasses your nostrils. For an avid fan, this moment is almost Utopian, as if you are setting foot on hallow ground. Once you realize that you are, in fact, still on Earth, you settle in to your seat and search for the nearest walking vendor, shouting about an assortment of refreshments for sale.

When the beer guy is within earshot, you find some money (likely more than you'd ever typically pay for a bottle of beer anywhere else) and call him over. Luckily, the beer vendor has a plethora of full cans and is able to pour a cold drink for you, as if he somehow knew you were going to order it. Realistically, though, he didn't know that you, specifically, would be there, thirsty and ready to root for your team. What he is aware of, however, is simple economics, the theory of supply and demand. The vendor had a can of beer (the supply) for fan's drinking needs during a football game (the demand). And that, my friends, is economics.

What is ec·o·nom·ics?

Ec·o·nom·ics (phonetically: *ek-uh-nom-iks*) is defined as "the science that deals with the production, distribution, and consumption of goods and services, or the material welfare of humankind." Like so many definitions that can sound daunting at first, this complex one can be dissected into digestible concepts and theories. After all, as promised, this book undertakes the task of simplifying economics so that anyone can understand the basic premise of economic theory.

People endure and employ different facets of economics each and every day without even knowing how an economic theory might apply to their situation. The examples used in this book are relative to many consumers, and the book applies specific theories to help you make sense of the way consumers buy and sell goods in the market.

As indicated by our example of the thirsty football fan, sporting events are just one occurrence filled with examples of economics, beginning with the entrance tickets and continuing to the wages of the after-game custodial crew. Though it is not always extremely apparent, economic theory occurs naturally every day. The relevancy of the examples in this book will help shed some light on the basic instances.

This book is not in any way intended to be a crash course in how supply and demand can be evaluated a million and one different ways. Rather, the goal here is to hopefully shed some positive light on economic theory and evaluation. Economics is a powerful tool that can help to explain a wide variety of events that plague the minds of people every day. For example, what would happen if milk prices increased exponentially over the period of a year? Would consumers switch to another source of calcium for their daily intake, or would they allocate more of their budget to fork out the higher price? Is there a price ceiling to cap off what consumers would be willing to pay for a gallon of milk? This book will thoroughly examine and dissect questions just like this one and will give you a better understanding of economics by bringing it to the forefront and opening your mind of its occurrence in your everyday life.

There tends to be some stigma attached to economics, as it is often mistakenly perceived to be "boring" or overly theoretical. As an economist, I will admit that some of the examples used in textbooks are completely inapplicable to real-life situations. My goal, therefore, is to help dismiss and dispel some of the negative connotations associated with economics. This book presents real-world examples that can help divulge a comprehendible explanation for economic theory.

Have you ever questioned why gas stations that are cater-cornered to one another advertise the same prices, right down to one-tenth of a cent? What incentivizes professional athletes to risk their personal health to consume performance-enhancing substances? Will massive taxes on cigarettes actually cause a large number of people in the United States to stop smoking, thereby increasing the quality of the country's overall health? Surely, there are a variety of answers and speculations to these questions, with justifications and arguments to support them, but in this book, you will find logical explanations and answers by peering at these issues through an economic lens.

This book is a compilation of interesting events, facts, data, and ramblings that introduce economic topics and theories in a matter-of-fact way. I want to reiterate that the examples used herein are logical questions that average people ask themselves every day. As you will see, many of the examples and theories are intertwined with one another. When they are not presented that way, it is still relatively simple to "connect the dots," so to speak, between theories. There are various similarities in economic theory that can be applicable in different contexts.

This book was inspired by the invigorating works of Steven Levitt and Stephen J. Dubner, creators of Freakonomics. After I read this book, I thought about the world differently. I began compiling some of the twisted events that encompass my day-to-day life and sprinkled in economic theory. This book is the culmination of those discoveries.

If you haven't read Freakonomics or its sequel, SuperFreakonomics, it would behoove you to put this book down and read both of them first. They are simply amazing resources, outstanding accounts of history, economics, and research, strategically woven into a comprehendible story. The authors have provoked much thought for me and for millions of others, and I am sure their work would be just as eye- and mind-opening to you.

Years after these two books were initially published, people are still writing in to the authors and participating in both structured and unstructured forums of discussion in various mediums. I chose to read these books amidst my temporary apathy for most written work back when I was in college. As an undergraduate, I was subjected to the overwhelming requirements of textbook reading, and there was so much reading that I was "forced" to do for class that the thought of reading for enjoyment was almost inconceivable. The fact that I couldn't put their books down, even in the midst of such a distaste for all things printed, is a testament to how interesting and beneficial the books are.

The two authors spent years researching and experimenting to uncover some of the anomalies contained in their books. They applied logic and economics to help explain some of the great wonders and historical occurrences. Though I was very encouraged by their written work, I feel it is important that you know that this book does not contain the same structure or analytical design; this book is a work all its own.

Although Steven Levitt and Stephen J. Dubner may never read this, I want to thank these two exceptional economists for inspiring me to "think outside the box," cliché as that may sound these days since the idiom is so overused. Instead of accepting the mundane normality that I face every day, I now question the function of these events and how economics is intertwined in everything we do. Clearly, this interests you too; hence, you are reading this book.

Before you dive deeply in, I want to warn you that this book—nor any book, for that matter—is not going to answer all of your questions regarding economics, if any. My goal here is to spark more questions and ultimately leave the answers up for interpretation. We will address questions, such as how people found alternate opportunities during the economic recession to provide for their families. It will provide perspective on why specific commodities like textbooks are so expensive. What impact does an individual's level of education have on their lifetime wage, as compared to someone with less educational background? This book will help to divulge an economically based answer to this question and others, but ultimately, it will open up your mind so that you can discern the answers for yourself. Most of the information presented has the potential for a variety of explanations. In fact, you will find that there are very few concrete black and white answers in these pages. It is my hope that you will not even be able to decipher between the two and that you will ponder the gray area that does, in fact, exist. Labeling things as "black or white" is a designation that infers that something is right or wrong, good or bad, positive or negative. In my opinion, this is not the case. I like to think there are always two sides to every story, argument, and discussion. There is always another opinion or a blend of two or more outlooks; this is the gray area. The foundation of this book is reliant on the fact that this so-called "gray area" is not only acceptable, but outright encouraged. I thrive on the notion of argumentative debates. To me, the gray area represents the ability of people to ponder both rational and irrational thought and for both to leverage equal tolerability for the sake of discussion. I challenge you to argue against my claims in the book if your opinion varies from mine. In fact, I would welcome the opportunity to discuss it with you!

Many of the topics you are about to read intertwine my personal opinion and biased account of specific occurrences from my past. It is almost impossible not to incorporate subjective information along with the arguments. However, the examples I chose to include can be applicable to almost anyone in society, my readers included. In other words, if you keep an open mind, somewhere in these pages, you will find something that is applicable in your situation and your life.

The information presented incorporates opinions from the perspective of an avid economist. I wrote these compilations to present another point of view and to shed a positive light on economic theory. My hope is that readers will discover that economic theory is not just a load of inapplicable concepts, the dull stuff of a required class in college; rather, economics is actually be relevant to the lives of most modern people, or at least stimulating to think about. I want people to question what I write and formulate their own opinions, and regardless of where you reside in that gray area on any of these issues, I sincerely hope you enjoy what you read.

Chapter One

Economists Want To Be "Better Off"

There is something important you should know about economists before you venture any further into this book. It is engrained within us to always want to be "better off." This means that regardless of a situation or decision, economists strive for the outcome to be slightly better than ever before. If an economist has the chance to increase to change their happiness level with relatively few complications, one can assume they will follow through with it. This is an assumption that can be made throughout every example in this entire book.

Economists measure their happiness with a designation of utility: The better something is from the perspective of a consumer, the higher the utility measure it yields. Candy, for example, has a relatively high utility meter for most people (including me). Why? Because candy is typically consumed by most people as a treat or a reward. The sugary sensation that tickles the taste buds has a positive effect on a person's overall gratification. Therefore, people usually eat candy to be "better off"; as a result, this increases the utility meter of the candy. This is also important to keep in mind as you continue reading.

Earning Some Extra Cash

My first encounter with modern behavioral economics stemmed from an e-mail I received during my tenure at Indiana University. It offered financial compensation to participate in an "experiment." I was a poor undergraduate student at the time, so it was only natural that I would respond cordially to such an enticing incentive to receive money in exchange for a mere hour of my time. Remember: Economists always want to be better off!

I arrived at the testing site in a building on campus, and a group of about twenty of my fellow peers accompanied me. When the group entered the testing room, we were given a specific set of instructions. The group would be divided into two subgroups, and every person in the room was blindly "paired" with someone from the other group. The administrator would project the next set of directions after we split. As a herd of us migrated to the next room, we were instructed to take a seat. The administrator then distributed envelopes filled with money to each participant.

We were told that we needed to make a decision concerning the money in the envelope: We could choose to keep all of the money for ourselves or give part or all of the money in the envelope to one of the people we were discretely "paired" with in the other room. The envelopes containing our decisions were anonymously given to our counterparts in the other group by the administrator. Once the second set of individuals received the envelopes, they had the choice of accepting or rejecting the money we gave them.

I dismissed my initial selfish thought to keep all of the money for myself. Instead, I tried to think of what decision would yield the greatest reward. Knowing it was some sort of psychological behavior test, I proceeded to donate all of the money in the experiment under the assumption that the more I theoretically "gave up," the higher the payout would be in the end. I assumed correctly.

At the time, I was merely interested in the money and dismissed any form of knowledge or experimental gain from my actions. As I later learned, this was a form of Game Theory that collected empirical data about decision-making.

The Prisoner's Dilemma: To Confess or To Deny

In economics, Game Theory involves the complex decisions one makes based on the actions of another individual or entity to ultimately maximize the payout one will receive. Game Theory is used to predict human behavior by organizing payout potentials in a matrix. One of the most famous Game Theory examples revolves around the decisions of criminals and is known as the "Prisoner's Dilemma."

In this game, two prisoners are arrested for the same crime and taken to be questioned in separate rooms. Neither has a chance to speak to the other, and each prisoner is looking to maximize their individual payoff. In this case, their goal is to receive the smallest amount of time in jail. The police display the matrix below to elucidate the penance structure for criminals. Both individuals have two choices: they can confess or deny their actions related to the crime. The mutually exclusive choices that the two must make influence the outcome of the other prisoner's fate.

		Prisoner A	
		Confess	Deny
Prisoner B	Confess	(-6, -6)	(0, -10)
	Deny	(-10, 0)	(-1, -1)

The matrix is a summary of the outcomes of each of the possible scenarios. If Prisoner A chooses to confess and Prisoner B chooses to deny, Prisoner A will receive no sentence, and Prisoner B goes to jail for ten years. If Prisoner B chooses to confess and Prisoner A chooses to deny, Prisoner B will receive no sentence, and Prisoner A will go to jail for ten years. If both prisoners choose to confess to the crime, both will receive a sentence, but it will only be for six years. Therefore, Prisoner B has an incentive to confess if and only if Prisoner A confesses, because Prisoner B's sentence will be four years shorter.

However, if both prisoners decide to deny the accusations, each individual receives only one year in jail. This gives the prisoners an incentive to cheat and deny the accusations in order to receive the smallest punishment, but if and only if the other prisoner denies the crime. Without knowing what the other prisoner is doing, theoretically both will choose to confess because the risk of denying the crime is far greater if the other person chooses to confess. It is essential to remember that in this form of the game, neither prisoner knows what the other is going to decide, as they are held in separate rooms and cannot communicate. Since both decisions are made simultaneously, the best choice is always to confess.

This is called the "dominant strategy" because it has the best outcome, regardless of what the other prisoner chooses. Because the individual is only concerned with his or her own outcome in this case, it is the only logical choice. It is also vital to note that the prisoners both know and understand the consequences they will face dependent on their choices. If both prisoners trust one another, they may take the risk that they will both choose to deny and mutually receive a better outcome.

The problem is that so-called "gentlemen's agreements" or verbal commitments with people are less than honorable. It is also critical to note that in this form of the game, it is assumed that the prisoners did not have time to discuss what they were going to do. Why would one prisoner trust that the other will not confess, when they are both aware of the available outcomes? The truth is that most people wouldn't trust the other, thus the concept of the Prisoner's Dilemma.

An assumption that needs to be noted in the Prisoner's Dilemma is that the concern is for any given moment in time. The theory does not take into account what occurred before the decision is made or what will happen after it; the decision time is the present. It is also vital to understand that this theory does not encompass all of the players in any given scenario. It is more centrally concentrated on specific markets. It usually involves only two distinct players or competitors who base their strategic planning on the decisions of the other.

There should be another supposition to ignore morality during the preceding examples of the Prisoner's Dilemma. The theory disregards any consideration of beliefs or values that one may experience. The examples should be taken literally, completely at face value. In other words, emotional or moral decision-making does not affect the outcome. This means that neither prisoner considers lying to be wrong in this scenario. The choice they make is based solely on reducing jail time. Economists care about maximizing the payout they will receive from confessing or not confessing. The matrix of payouts does not change in any example of the Prisoner's Dilemma because all forms of personalization are removed.

The Cold War

The explanation presented is theoretical in nature, but there are various accounts in history and the present that embody the Prisoner's Dilemma. The first reverts back to the 1940s, during World War II, in a period when a lot of very rash changes occurred between the two sides. Toward the latter part of the war, the Soviet Union formed a temporary alliance with the Allies, aligning with them to defeat Germany. Once this cumbersome task became more of a reality, the two partners each retained vastly different ideals for control in the future. Needless to say, the newly formed political ties did not last long.

Near the end of the war, tension grew between the United States and the Soviet Union. The two sides clashed in their political opinions and invariably argued over occupational territory of the newly defeated land. The United States and the Allies remained closely tied to Western Europe, while the Soviet Union controlled Eastern Europe to protect neighboring countries.

Under the fierce leadership of Joseph Stalin, the Soviet Union's control grew to become known as the Eastern Bloc, and it included a vast majority of bordering satellite states to the Soviet Union. The Allies saw this new conglomerate as a threat to the Western world and identified the ongoing and growing tension between the two world forces. Little did anyone know that this threat would amount to six decades of war between the two enemies.

Between 1945 and 1946, the Cold War began between

the Allies and the Soviets. The Cold War centered on a conglomeration of war propaganda, military coalitions, technological competitions, and conventional and nuclear arms races between both sides. Both forces began collecting and accumulating war weaponry, though neither ever initiated direct physical attacks or fighting. You might wonder why this history lesson is so important. The Cold War appears to have little or nothing to do with behavioral economics, until the Prisoner's Dilemma theory is applied.

The Cold War was ultimately a vast assemblage of a wide variety of war propaganda for each side rather than typical direct-war battles with man-to-man fighting. The hands-off nature of the Cold War replaced actual battles with sizeable amounts of military arms. Each side fought to build larger, more destructive weapons, always trying to one-up the opposition's stockpile. According to the Prisoner's Dilemma, both the Soviets and the United States chose to "confess" by publicly building up their militia and ammo.

Each side was well aware of the outcome of participation or lack thereof of their opponents. If the Soviets increased the propaganda and military stockpile, it would be extremely risky for the United States not to do the same. After all, an equal increase of military arms eliminates the power distinction among the two sides. If the U.S. did not increase their military hoard, the world military force risked a possible invasion or attack from their counterpart and vice versa. Therefore, they had to keep up with the enemy and counteract the move. Paralleling the Prisoner's Dilemma, it is all about the outcome matrix and how to maximize the best possible outcome in the situation.

In order to dive further into the Prisoner's Dilemma, let's take a closer look at a specific arms battle, since one of the most impactful historical accounts during the Cold War deeply encompasses the Prisoner's Dilemma. The Soviet Union united with the Cubans when the United States severed ties with the country. The Cubans received word of a possible U.S. attack and retaliated to the reports with what became known as the Cuban Missile Crisis.

With the help of the Soviets, the Cubans constructed a nuclear missile to use as military propaganda against the United States. To follow suit (as within the Prisoner's Dilemma), the United States entered into the nuclear arms race to see which power could generate the largest amount of military propaganda (each side wanted to maximize their potential payout).

There were no actual battles in the Cold War because it was purely based on the Prisoner's Dilemma concept. The actions of each force enticed the other to automatically choose to "confess" or get involved in the nuclear arms race because the payoff was better (and safer) than ignoring it. If either side ignored the opposition, they posed the risk of being attacked by a larger military stockpile. Tensions revolved around the countries, causing each to become entangled in war. In order to maximize the payout, each side participated.

Looking at this from another standpoint, the safest choice would have been for both to "deny" or not become involved with nuclear weapons at all, dude to the obvious consequences of this dangerous propaganda. Each side could have made a gentlemen's agreement to avoid the wartime era. Unfortunately, officials on both sides felt they had to protect their borders, and since there was a perceived risk that the opposition might not hold up their end of the bargain, each side became trapped. Remember: Morality does not apply to decision-making. The Prisoner's Dilemma (and this example) illustrate that economic theory does not factor trusted gentlemen's agreements into the equation. The threat of military propaganda is far too significant of a risk to base anything on a meager handshake or word of mouth.

Why Is It Advantageous for Tobacco Companies to Invest Billions of Dollars on Advertising?

A second example of the Prisoner's Dilemma directly relates to a commodity used by about 34 percent of the world's population: cigarettes. Globally, the industry generates approximately $400 billion each year. In the United States alone, there are nearly

48.2 million smokers. One would think that with this kind of remarkable user retention and revenue, cigarette manufacturers must have exceptional advertising and marketing teams to reach such a scope of consumers. Surely these marketing teams must have some magical algorithm that outlines the perfect advertising scheme in order to generate the monstrosity of revenue of the tobacco business, right? Wrong!

Historically, cigarette advertisements appealed to consumers on emotional terms. The ads integrated a positive self-identity with the product. Men who chose to smoke were illustrated as "more masculine" than nonsmokers, and men with a cigarette in their hand were portrayed as more desirable to the ladies. Not only was this acceptable at the time, but the attractiveness associated with users of the product was the norm.

On the contrary, long, thin cigarettes consumed mainly by women appealed to the "ultra-feminine" aura that users portrayed with the product in hand. The specialty of the shape and size of the product mimicked the "ideal" female figure. As I was doing my research, I found two advertisements that directly exemplify this concept.

For example, the women in the ads were gorgeous, with flowing blonde hair, glistening bright-colored eyes, and the perfected waist measurements of a plastic doll. The women were surrounded by paparazzi that jumped at the chance to snap a few pictures of the model-like figure. The women emitted a flawless aura that fueled the desire of every man she laid her eyes on. The women elegantly held the elongated cigarette as an additional accessory to make her even more glamorous. Women who consumed these cigarettes retained a charm that was associated with the product. This enticed consumers to purchase the particular brand.

Although these ideals catered to the American public in the past, industry standards and regulations have since dramatically altered the appeal of the product. The future of the industry became severely volatile, and the companies merely adhered to the Prisoner's Dilemma to maximize the best possible outcome.

As the industry further evolved and the government's involvement increased, cigarette manufacturers experienced intense scrutiny regarding the harmful effects of their products. Although negative health accusations regarding the products are warranted (cancer and other potentially fatal diseases have been linked to tobacco consumption), many of the leading tobacco manufacturers have had to comply with strict federal and state regulations to manufacture and distribute their products.

One of the most impactful pieces of legislation for these companies (and the source for the Prisoner's Dilemma in this example) outlines when, where, and how tobacco manufacturers go to market. In 1998, the Master Settlement Agreement (MSA) was a conglomeration of multiple lawsuits between the attorney general of forty-six states and the four largest tobacco companies in the industry. The companies were required to follow strict regulations in order to continue to merchandise and sell their products on the market. The legislation demanded that the tobacco companies also pay an ongoing annual fee to cover state and federally funded healthcare costs relating to tobacco use. The additional provisions restricted advertising methods for the products.

The tobacco companies were now prohibited from advertising their products in public mediums that were readily available to all citizens. More specifically, advertisements had to be limited to target demographics of people over the age of eighteen. The number of regulations and restrictions placed on marketing in the industry skyrocketed. As such, the marketing teams at the tobacco companies were forced to adjust their advertising techniques to comply.

The Prisoner's Dilemma is applied differently to this example. The restriction was not on advertising itself, but more on the medium that the companies used to project the features of their products to consumers. Public forums such as magazines, billboards, television commercials, sponsored sporting events, and free samples vanished as viable means to reach customers. Instead, the companies had to develop other means to send messages to consumers. Because of the limited number of large competitors in the oligopolistic tobacco market, the firms watched their rivals meticulously for comparison.

The cigarette manufacturing companies were faced with a significant and weighty decision: What would be the most impactful medium by which they could advertise to connect directly with cigarette consumers? The answer was unclear. Due to the nature of the product, there was a negative connotation associated with the sale of tobacco products. Ultimately, tobacco companies had to change their methods of advertising. They began gathering a plethora of information about the consumers of the product so they could gear their advertising methods to reap the best results. Their research led them to the realization that their largest physical space to directly connect with consumers was via retail outlets. This became the premise of the Prisoner's Dilemma for this example.

In spite of how it had been advertised in the past as something glamorous and masculine, tobacco, as a commodity, quickly became taboo in the market. Sales were centralized in a handful of retail locations including convenience stores, supermarkets, liquor stores, and tobacco stores. Cigarette sales accounted for approximately 30 percent of total annual convenience store revenue. In other words, retail owners needed to partner with tobacco companies because the sales represented such a huge piece of their business. The companies began incentivizing retail merchants to advertise the products for them, offering copious compensation for limited space in the store. The largest physical area per square foot landed directly on the cigarette fixture. Surprisingly, the government's many restrictions did not include such advertising space.

Large cigarette manufacturers developed contracts and plan-o-grams that precisely assigned homes for each brand portfolio. This was based on volume percentages of past sales. For example, if a store sold 60 percent of Brand A overall, the store was expected to merchandise Brand A on 60 percent of the fixture. Not only were stores paid to merchandise the product, but also to provide extra allowances to drive down the price to consumers.

This created a competitive advantage in retail for those stores that complied with the requests of the cigarette manufacturers. Ultimately, these stores had better (lower) prices and paralleling higher volumes. By designating specific brand percentages and slotting of items, certain companies and brands received a greater square footage of product on the shelf. This left some products to be merchandised in a non-visible area for a lack of space.

This caused a real dilemma, both literally and figuratively. Was it profitable for companies to invest the additional money in this form of advertising versus other methods? The answer is yes, but to what extent? The top tobacco companies began vigorously partnering with retail in hopes of making the largest impact. For example, tobacco companies enticed retailers with dollar figures of additional funds. This was sold to retail as a financial benefit to the store owner. If Company A decided to incentivize retail with a ten-dollar-per-carton allowance on the top brand, they would experience a significant lift in sales of that specific product.

According to the Prisoner's Dilemma, Company B was better off countering the incentive to follow the actions of Company A. If Company B chose not to reduce the price, consumers were financially incentivized to choose Company A's brand, resulting in a decline in Company B's profit. If both companies chose to participate in the reduced price strategy, they would both see an incremental increase in sales, though it would be slightly less than if only one company ran the sale.

This appeared to be a win-win-win situation for everyone: Consumers received a better price, retail owners increased volume and their bottom line, and cigarette manufacturers increased brand awareness through additional sales. The hidden side of this drastic change in advertising was the significant increase in advertising costs associated with the individual store marketing strategy. Both retailers and cigarette companies strived to generate a profit. In order to do so, they scrutinized how much profit was actually accrued after the significant investment in contractual retail agreements. Unfortunately, this alternative to traditional advertising was much more costly than originally anticipated.

According to the Prisoner's Dilemma, either company would suffer if the other "confessed" or spent more money on advertising and promoting. The suffering company would lose sales from price-sensitive consumers who would be willing to temporarily switch brands. In order to remain competitive, the largest companies invested billions of dollars to retain the customers who were loyal to their brands and the partnerships they had built with retail outlets.

According to the United States Center for Disease Control, in 2006, cigarette companies spent $12.4 billion on advertising and promotional expenses in the United States. This equated to more than double what was spent in 1997. In this case, it is vital for one company to follow suit to what the competition is doing. Thus, the battle rages on, an ongoing struggle.

Cigarette promotions have recently been more demographically and geographically focused. There are two main reasons for this. First, brand and flavor loyalty in the cigarette industry is greatly determined by the people in the specific area. In other words, specific geographies are heavily dominated by certain brands. Many people experience their first cigarette by "bumming" one off of a friend, though this is not always the case, for there is always that one consumer who ventures into their local convenience store and uses the close-your-eyes-and-point method to choose a pack at random; but in the first case, the brand one smoker smokes will likely be the same brand the other smoker smokes. According to the Center for Disease Control, every single day, about 3,450 young people between 12 and 17 years pick up their first cigarette, and many of these young people follow in the footsteps of their peers, right down to the brand their friends smoke.

In other words, if someone's friend happens to smoke a menthol flavor of Brand A, chances are that the new smoker will end up smoking the same flavor and brand. People inherently trust others and associate that trust with the products another person uses. Therefore, large geographical areas tend to have trends of similarity.

These trends depict pockets of promotional opportunities for the cigarette companies. Again, this reverts back to the Prisoner's Dilemma. Large tobacco companies will promote specific flavors and brands in areas that are highly concentrated with those flavors.

For example, Brand C is a menthol flavor and is exceptionally successful in a given market. Brand C's largest competitor, Brand A in a menthol flavor, is deeply discounted and integrated into the market. If consumers have already proven that they like the menthol variety of Brand C, those price-conscious consumers will try the highly discounted Brand A. Following the theory, Brand C must develop a discounted program to follow suit and share the boosted volume.

The second reason for demographical and geographical promotions is due to federal, state, and city taxes that impose large burdens (with minimal consumer gains, which will be discussed more in Chapter 3) on tobacco users. For example, in the Chicago market, a pack of cigarettes retails for an average of $8.50. Approximately 50 percent of this consumer cost is tax. Because taxes are generally determined by geographical laws, this significantly contributes to promotional activity.

In order to offer the consumers in these areas a deal to purchase the product, cigarette companies develop "test markets." Growth stems from trial on new products in the market. Because new products sell with introductory price points, special discounts on new items for increased incentive of trial, taxes are not perceived as much of a burden to consumers, who are more concerned with the end price. This is also a benefit for tobacco companies, because they are able to gain advertising knowledge, consumer insights, and preemptive volume sales on innovative products by testing them first. Consumer demand drives market trends, while price is typically dictated more often by suppliers. Gasoline is another prime example of this concept.

A Penny Saved Is Much More Than a Penny Earned

The current national average price of regular unleaded gasoline in 2011 was $3.61 per gallon, as compared to the 2010 average of $2.67. This is an increase of 35.2 percent for a single commodity, something that did not improve to warrant an increase. As exemplified from these simple statistics, gas prices are one of the most extremely volatile variables in a given time period. Other commodities are lucky to increase at the rate of inflation (which tends to hover around 3 percent per year), without the general public griping about the escalated price.

Just to show how drastic of an increase this is, I would like to use milk (a standard commodity) as a comparative example. An average gallon of milk retailed between $3.50 and $3.99 in 2011. If milk prices inflated at the same rate as gas, prices in 2012 would run between $4.73 and $5.39 per gallon, surely resulting in a lot of outraged consumers and some cocky cows! Although a few outliers would purchase milk despite the cost, the majority of consumers would try to find another source of calcium.

Price sensitivity of gas is so extreme that advertisements go to the extent of listing $3.619 instead of $3.62. With a multitude of gas stations readily available within a one-mile radius of most urban markets, consumers have a choice of where to purchase their gasoline. Many four-corner intersections have a different gas station on each corner. The managers of these facilities are obsessive about checking competitive prices and maintaining equality down to the penny (and sometimes one-tenth of a penny!). Why is this strategy so extreme? Gas stations within a relatively close geography experience the Prisoner's Dilemma.

Regular unleaded gasoline standards require specific chemicals to fuel an engine in a car. The United States government sets regulations for the quality standards of this commodity. Because of this, the brand of the same grade of gasoline is something many consumers do not consider when purchasing. Branding is irrelevant when there is little to no quality differentiation between two distinct venues.

Keeping this in mind, consider the consequences if one gas station, Station A, in a competitive intersection dropped their price by two cents per gallon. In other words, they chose to "confess" in this case. Because the stations in the intersection are within 200 feet of one another, location is negligible; a consumer can easily choose to drive to either station without a major inconvenience. Why would any consumer choose to go to the higher-priced gas station for the exact same commodity? They won't!

Station B, in the same intersection, has the option to "confess" and lower their price by the same amount or to "deny" and compete with a higher price. By "denying," they will ultimately sabotage their revenue because the same commodity can be purchased for less money right next door. Any rational consumer will gravitate toward the two-cent savings. As a result, Station B has a larger incentive to follow the Prisoner's Dilemma and "confess" (or lower the price).

There are two distinct impetuses for retail to lower prices. First, there is a larger perceived savings than just two cents per gallon. One might argue that Station B risks losing that additional two cents per gallon in revenue by lowering the price. This is true, but the loss is taken with a potential larger marginal gain. Although that two cents might appear to be a menial discount, price-conscious consumers are accustomed to equivalent pricing amongst gas-selling competitors. Even the slightest discount per gallon is perceived to be a great savings for the overall purchase.

With the latest technology implemented through the Internet and Smartphone applications, consumers now have direct access to a plethora of gas prices in a given area. The website GasBuddy. com provides users with an opportunity to look up the price of gas at different stations in an area. This makes competition even more difficult.

Not only does the website provide consumers with prices down to the penny, but it also gives a direct option to map the location from where the consumer is located. For someone who is unfamiliar with the area, the website provides a simplistic method to find the cheapest possible commodity. This creates a price sensitive market at the fingertips of consumers. Because of tools like this one, retail owners need to be especially accommodating if they want to snag the business of their price-conscious consumers.

There is a second function of penny savings on gas: Consumers tend to associate discounted prices with the establishment as a whole. In other words, if an establishment advertises that they have "discounted gas," the reputation of the store will allude to a discount atmosphere. It isn't coincidental that outdoor price signs show a tenth of a cent. This is strategic, an attempt to portray some sort of savings (even if it is a mere penny or less) to the consumer. Gasoline is a commodity that yields a few pennies, if any, per sale. The real dollar margins are made on commodities for sale inside the walls of the store.

If a customer is hungry, thirsty, or needing lotto tickets or cigarettes while they are pumping gas, they are likely to purchase convenience items, and these yield margins of 25 to 60 percent from the same store. The key to success is to lure customers into the gas station. While they are there, and especially if they have to go inside to pay for their gas, many will make impulsive purchases of items with huge profit margins. With statistics like that, Station B has a significant incentive to lower their price (or confess). If they don't, they risk a much larger loss than two cents. They risk losing the loyalty of a customer. This directly embodies the Prisoner's Dilemma theory.

Consider another situation that many people can associate closely with: finding a place to live. The reason I have opted to use this as an example is because it is pure proof of how time plays a significant role in decision-making. Every person needs a dwelling. Because of economic downturn, many post-recession consumers looked to rent their homes instead of buying one, an attempt to protect their financial future from the burden of another recession or financial blow.

Homeowners that have the ability to rent to others are very cautious when considering who they will rent their property to.

It is critical for an owner to check credit scores and past financial history, acquire references, and build trust with the potential renters. Because of all of these criteria, renting is not as feasible and careless as it once was. There are a plethora of protective mechanisms that need to be checked before either party signs the lease.

This makes renting a difficult process. With the overabundance of homes that became available during and after the recession of 2008, the housing industry became a buyer's market. In other words, there was a massive supply of houses for sale with a relatively low demand. Because of this phenomenon, homeowners turned to renting.

For an example, let's assume that a young individual wants to rent a house or condominium for a fairly high rate in the market. Although this person is financially stable enough to purchase a home, they have a strong preference to rent. After all, renting has no long-term implications or commitments attached to it as a mortgage does. This person is even willing to pay more monthly rent to forego some of the expensive responsibilities of a home. The person will agree to sign a one-year lease to allow them leverage to move once the year of payment is complete.

The person searches the market and ads to identify the perfect living quarters. There is an average-priced condominium with a "For Sale" sign posted out front. Due to the market conditions and the lack of buyers in the market, the renter decides to take a look at the home anyway and tell the owner upfront that the intention is for rental. The homeowner agrees to show the condominium to the prospective tenant. The seller is hopeful that the renter likes the property so much that they will agree to purchase it instead of renting it.

In such a situation, the seller is under a time constraint because they have already purchased their next house and they have exactly two months to find a buyer (or renter) for their current property. They agree to renting as an option if they do not sell the property during the two-month timeframe.

When the renter takes a look at the property, they love it

and expresses their desire to sign a lease for the condominium. Because the property is currently not "for rent," the person continues to seek other suitable rental properties. The renter is upfront and honest about the possibility of renting another property because of the lack of commitment from this particular seller. The seller is now faced with the Prisoner's Dilemma.

The seller can choose to either rent the property or wait to sell it. Because they do not know if another buyer is going to approach them with an offer within the time allotment, they face a bit of a dilemma. There is no guarantee that any further offers will come. If they choose to rent (to "confess"), they will have a steady one-year income once the lease is signed. This money is guaranteed, but they will still own the property and be responsible for it. This is a positive outcome for the seller, but not the best possible option (because the seller's goal is still to sell the place).

On the contrary, the seller has the ability to dismiss the rental offer. This means the seller would wait and see if someone else wants to purchase the condominium (to "deny") in the two-month (or longer) window of time. The seller could still rent the property to the renter if the place does not sell within the given timeframe. In this case, the seller runs the risk of the renter accepting another lease offer for a different property. If another buyer does not approach the seller with an offer, they are much worse off than they would have been if they'd accepted the original rental offer, as they would be stuck with the responsibility of the mortgage.

In the downward spiraling housing market, the likelihood that another person would produce an offer for them is relatively slim. This relevant example occurs often, and even more so post-recession. The difficulty is that people still have the optimism that the purchasing offer they are seeking will eventually come their way.

The final example that I will adhere to the Prisoner's Dilemma revolves around an American pastime that motivates people to freeze out in negative three-degree weather in the heart of winter, frivolously spend money on inflated tickets (which will be discussed more in Chapter 6), and induce a sore throat from screaming at a television monitor. The pastime is football. And as an avid Chicago Bears fan, these have been firsthand experiences for me.

As a fan, I expect the Monsters of the Midway to charge onto the field every game and play their hearts out. I want players to perform each and every game. I would even venture to say that my expectations are unrealistic. I do not see the Bears as regular men, but hardworking soldiers who are capable of superhuman strength. Unfortunately, some of the players hold themselves to the same standards, to the point of compromising their better judgment or even their health.

Why do Professional Sports Players Offer Incentives to Use Performance-Enhancing Drugs?

The National Football League (NFL) has had a history of record-breaking games. Some of the players' accomplishments are absolutely unbelievable, and I mean that literally. Players have achieved goals that were well beyond expectations, and these players have been considered the epitome of perfect in the sport. Earning the title of an NFL professional football player comes with much responsibility. As pressure to be the best builds up, some players have turned to performance-enhancing supplements to push their bodies to the limit.

In 1987, the NFL began drug-testing players to determine if they were partaking of performance-enhancing supplements. Because the NFL wanted to deter players from harming their bodies, the use of these harmful drugs was prohibited. The most common performance-enhancing supplement used amongst players was the anabolic steroid, used to boost muscle strength and stamina that players could not normally achieve from weight training and practice. The drug helped them to run faster, tackle harder, jump higher, and retain enough energy for all four quarters and maybe even overtime.

As more and more players saw other individuals breaking records and achieving unthinkable feats, the pressure was on (and in some cases still is) for them to outperform their competitors.

Every player wants to go down in history and be remembered as the greatest running back, quarterback, defensive lineman, or tight end, and some will go to excessive lengths to achieve that goal.

This reverts back to the Prisoner's Dilemma. For this example, let's assume Players A and B are both ranked equally, tied for first place as the top linebacker in the NFL. If Player A decides to take performance-enhancing drugs, he should theoretically gain more strength than Player B. If Player A does not take any drugs, he risks Player B outperforming him on the field because of his supplemental enhancements. Player A has to look at the best outcome, which results in him taking the enhancement himself.

Player B also has the choice to take the substance (to "confess") or to not take it (to "deny"). Because Player A will have the competitive advantage over Player B when the outcome matrix proves to yield a higher payout with use of the enhancing drugs, Player B has more incentive to use the substance. If Player B chooses not to, Player A will have an automatic advantage over Player B. Player B will choose to confess and use the drug. This will help to level the competition and make them equal once again.

Although this is merely a theoretical example, it is extremely relevant in the race to become the best. Professional athletes experience tremendous pressure to outperform their counterparts on other teams. Competition is engrained in human instinct, and this is reinforced with weekly stats and rankings plastered all over sports network television. There have been numerous cases across a variety of sports teams of team members using these drugs to become the best.

Major League Baseball (MLB) had the famous "home-run race," in which players competed to break the record for the highest number of home-runs hit in one season. Many of the players competing for this honor tested positive for steroids or other enhancement drugs. The incentive to take the steroids (to confess) outweighed losing to a better-performing competitor.

The problem with the Prisoner's Dilemma is that it only considers what occurs in the current moment. The best possible outcomes are purely instant, and they tend to change within the next minute. The difference with this example is that it involves real people. As an advocate of professional sports, I do not endorse the use of these or any other synthetic substances to improve athletic performance. In this case, economic theory speaks for itself.

As proven, the Prisoner's Dilemma is applicable in a variety of contexts. Within each, it is critical to consider one's decisions based on what others will do. In most of these examples, economic theory speaks for itself in the decision-making process.

Chapter Two

Selfishless

Let's revisit my initial encounter of mingling psychological behavior with economic theory in the "money in envelope" experiment. Although the theoretical experiment I participated in was not the Prisoner's Dilemma, it involved a payout matrix and a choice. My choice to share the money in the envelope paid off. There was a designated pay scale that regimented the actual amount of money each subject would receive based on their previous decision to keep or share part of their initial payment.

Unlike the Prisoner's Dilemma, I was unaware of the structure of the payout matrix before my decision was made. It turns out that subjects who donated larger portions of the payouts were compensated at higher rates, and those who kept part or all of the money were compensated at significantly reduced rates. My altruistic thought process paid off, and I received the highest payout offered during the experiment. Coincidentally, my donation decision was actually the antithesis of altruistic.

Altruism is defined as "the principle or practice of unselfish concern for or devotion to the welfare of others." As I previously stated, I strategically thought through a potential payout matrix before I donated the complete amount of money in my initial envelope. Essentially, this was just a guess, but I had a strong feeling that the compensation for a complete donation yielded a higher final payout. Even if my instincts had been completely off kilter, I would still have been better off, having a miniscule gain of something rather than nothing.

Essentially, I was completely selfish in determining how I

achieve the highest payout. I actively made a conscious decision to determine how I thought this process would occur. By outwardly giving up the money in my envelope, I appeared to share my wealth by redistributing it to the stranger in the next room. To the naked eye, it would appear as though my "selfless" decision to donate all of the money to my opponent followed the theory of inequity aversion.

The Theory of Inequity Aversion

The theory of "inequity aversion," first studied by economists in 1978, is the preference for fairness and resistance to incidental inequalities between two parties. Preliminary experiments indicated that individuals felt a sense of "guilt" for unequal or unjust compensation. This emotion coerced them into sharing the financial gains with their opponents in the experiments. Unfortunately, I cannot take credit for being a selfless martyr who gives up all compensation to make others happy. At the time, I was just a college student trying to earn some extra cash.

I actively thought about the person in the other room and the reaction they were going to have. If I gave them a minute amount of money, they would reject the deal, which would result in very little or nothing given to me in return. As an economist, I am always looking to be better off. Even if that person would have only given me a dollar, I still would have been a dollar wealthier than I was before the experiment. Therefore, I sent all of the initial money to my counterpart in the other room.

This was a two-part game. I made one decision, and the person then considered my decision in order to make theirs. Unlike the Prisoner's Dilemma, the two players were not making simultaneous decisions. If it was like the Prisoner's Dilemma and I had to make that decision, my choice would have drastically changed: I would have kept all of the money.

Similar to everyday decisions, economics depends on circumstances and the sum of all parts of the equation. I walked away from that experiment with the largest amount of money that

I could have received. I rationalized the information that I knew and anticipated the outcome. Ultimately, it turned out to be a profitable walk to campus for me, and I utilized economic theory to achieve it.

Chapter Three

Gas-Guzzling Goods

In the previous two chapters, we've discussed gasoline as a commodity that has a variable range of prices in a relatively short period of time. Gasoline consumers are very price sensitive. Between 2010 and 2011, prices increased by 35.2 percent, yet consumers still purchased the product. Don't get me wrong: There are plenty of complaints, opinionated newspaper articles, and blogs ranting about the ever-growing prices, but when does this bubble of inflation subside and provide customers with relief? I have bad news: Unless you purchase a bike or an electric car, your gas costs are likely going to be on the rise for some time.

Gasoline is a commodity that people perceive as a need. When I fill up my tank, I categorize a trip to the gas station as another chore, similar to purchasing groceries. It's not something I want to spend my money on, but I have to. Why? Because, probably like you, I use my car to travel to work, run errands, and go to social events. Essentially, people in the United States have developed a need for gasoline to function normally unless they reside in a highly urbanized, small geographical location that does not require them to travel any distance.

Gasoline has two important functions in society: efficiently moving people from Point A to Point B in various forms of transportation within a reasonable amount of time and enabling people to get to work so that they can earn money. For this example, let's assume most people need some form of employment to sustain the basic necessities of food, water, clothing, and shelter. Now that we have established a need for gas, what differentiates this product from others to the point where consumers consent to pay the exceptionally inflated prices? The difference is that gas has a relatively inelastic demand.

Elastic Goods Versus Inelastic Goods

The elasticity of a product's demand says a lot about that product. Goods are said to be either elastic or inelastic based on the market demand as the price changes. Goods are considered to be more elastic when a slight change in price results in a sharp change in demand. This can be positive or negative, and the concept is explained more thoroughly using a graphical illustration.

In the graph below, consider Points A and B. If the price for an elastic good drops dramatically and goes from Point A to Point B, there will be a significant increase in the number of consumers who are willing to purchase the item. The quantity demanded at Point B is much more than the quantity at Point A. On the other hand, if the price of the item quickly increases moving from Point B up to Point A, the demand for the good will greatly decline. The quantity demanded at Point A is much less than the quantity demanded at Point B.

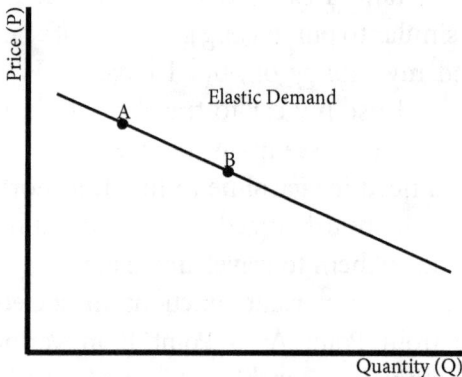

Let's use the milk example from Chapter 1 to describe the behavior patterns of an elastic good. As stated in the previous chapter, most people could purchase a gallon of milk in the United States for between $3.50 and $3.99 per gallon in 2011.

If the price of this good increased at the same increase rate of gasoline for 2012, it would cost a person between $4.73 and $5.39 per gallon. As the price goes up in this example from Point B (2011) to Point A (2012), there will be a significant decline in the quantity of gallons of milk demanded. Logically speaking, most consumers would refuse to pay such a price for this good since it is not an essential need for them to live.

As an alternative, people have the option to substitute soy milk or other calcium-enriched products and still receive the desired vitamins and nutrients. This is one of the classifying characteristics of elastic goods. Substitution of other products renders price increases irrelevant to the consumer, and consumers have a choice to spend less money on the same product. As a result, the quantity demanded of the product decreases.

The other classification of a good based on a price change is inelasticity. If a good is considered to be inelastic, a significant change in price has relatively little to no effect on the quantity demanded of the good and can also be positive or negative. In the graph below, consider Points A and B.

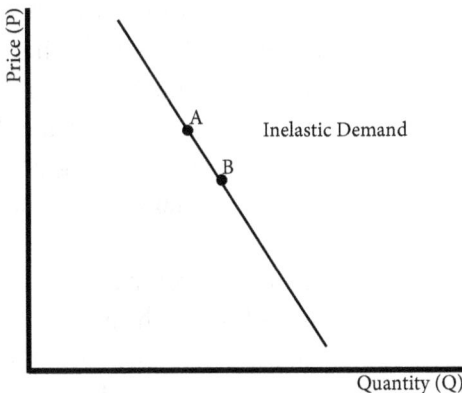

If the price for an inelastic good drops dramatically and goes from Point A to Point B, there is not a significant increase in the number of consumers who are willing to purchase the item. The quantity demanded at Point B is not that much more than the quantity at Point A. This is because the demand of the inelastic good has a much steeper slope than elastic goods.

On the other hand, if the price of the item quickly increases moving from Point B up to Point A, the demand for the good remains about the same. The quantity demanded at Point A is very similar the quantity demanded at Point B.

One of the best examples of an inelastic good is the gasoline we discussed earlier. Gasoline prices can vary significantly over a period of time. If someone owns a car that functions as their main transportation on a daily basis, a ninety-four-cent per gallon increase in price (the actual increase noted earlier from 2010 to 2011) will not incentivize them to sell their car. One reason for this is that there is not a direct substitute for fuel in cars. While some newer-model cars and hybrids will run on other types of power and fuel, for the most part, cars will not run on other substances besides gasoline.

If someone stopped purchasing this commodity because of a change in price, they would have to figure out another method of transportation that does not involve gasoline. For example, a bicycle is significantly less efficient (in most cases) and would not suffice as a suitable substitute. It cannot provide the same outcome as a car can because of the shorter distance that it travels in the same period of time. A bike rider would have to allow significantly more time for travel which could be used to work, enabling them to earn the price difference of gas. People have become accustomed to relying on the utility of cars. Because of this theory, the demand for gasoline does not change significantly, even when the price increases or decreases. Consumers gripe about the higher cost, but they will still pay it because they consider it a need for which there is no alternative.

Other factors can also influence the elasticity of goods. Individual consumer perception of need is largely integrated in the elasticity of a good. For example, water is a basic human necessity; as a result, it is an inelastic good. For a marathon runner who just finished a 26.2-mile race, water is much more relatively inelastic than it is for an office worker sitting stagnant at their desk. The runner needs to replenish the lost fluids in a timely manner, and their lack of energy does not allow them the option of waiting for a drink. There are also almost no substitutes that would provide the pure water the runner's body requires. On the contrary, the office worker would merely be quenching their thirst, so any other suitable drink would suffice. Thus, water becomes much less inelastic. One could even venture to say that for the office worker, water could become slightly elastic if the person finds a substitute that they are equally happy with at the time. The thirsty office worker is in need of a beverage off some sort, not water in particular. This is how the elasticity of a good can vary depending on the level of need behind it.

Elasticity and Substitutable Goods

Aside from alternative substitutes of similar products, there is another channel to consider with elastic goods: the private label sector. Private label brands are those distributed by retailers under their own banner but produced by other manufacturers. Although retailers may merchandise the nationally recognized brands, thousands of stores carry their own private label of a multitude of diverse items under their own distinct brand names. Most retail outlets use the name of their larger corporation for the goods.

There are thousands of items sold under generic brand names, produced by various manufacturers worldwide. Limited advertising costs, generic packaging, and bulk quantities contribute to retailer savings and the ability to offer a lower price to consumers while simultaneously turning a profit. Corporations are incentivized to offer these items because of the significant percentage increase in profit margin that they make as opposed to the national brand.

A challenge for retailers is to figure out the elasticity of a private label product versus the national brand. The private label offering is a direct substitute for this product. It is produced and merchandised to mimic the national brand. For this reason, it is called a perfect substitute. This means that the demand of the private label increases as the price of the national brand increases. This happens because consumers recognize this product as an equal to the national brand. The task is determining how to price both to prevent cannibalization of either of the two products.

So how does all of this apply to actual market changes? I want to apply the elasticity of demand to two distinct types of products in the market: tobacco and prescription drugs. Although these are vastly different goods, they play a key role in the market because of the nature of each. First, let's revisit tobacco and discuss its inherent trends.

As mentioned in Chapter 1, tobacco is a substance that receives great scrutiny from consumers, the government, and critics. The number of lawsuits associated with the product seems to grow exponentially each year. It is no secret that tobacco can be harmful, and it is highly addictive because of the nicotine the products contain. We've already established that consumers of the product are typically extraordinarily loyal to their brand, and it is one of the largest consumable goods in the world. Because of these characteristics, tobacco is a very unique product.

For the following example, we will discuss cigarettes as the tobacco product in the market. Similar to prohibition in the 1920s, the product is classified as a "sinful" good. Although it has never been banned, federal and state laws focus largely on protection from its negative side effects. Thus, the United States government places cumbersome excise taxes on these goods. These "sin taxes" have various purposes.

Government Incentives to Keep Tobacco Legalized

To provide a better understanding of the brevity of these taxes, I looked up exactly how much one 2009 tax increase changed the price of cigarettes. These taxes are determined by the Alcohol and Tobacco Tax Trade Bureau and are levied by the federal government.

In a single tax increase in April of 2009, regular cigarette taxes increased from $0.39 per pack to $1.01 per pack—a 159 percent increase in taxes alone! Consumers and retailers were naturally outraged by this jump, but what was the government's reasoning behind these massive increases in tax burdens for the consumers that use tobacco products?

I was under the assumption that the government levies these taxes to motivate people to stop smoking and ultimately decrease the number of smokers in the United States. This would imply that the government's goal is to improve the overall health of the American public. Prior to my theoretical education (specifically in economics), I embraced this notion because it seemed to make logical sense. Keep in mind through this explanation that I am a nonsmoker, so my preconceived assumptions were admittedly that of a nonsmoker before I learned about the product.

Any rational thinker could infer that an increase in price of a good will cause fewer people to consume it. The previous milk example holds this assumption to be true. If the price of milk went up drastically to ten dollars a gallon on a whim, people would substitute other substances for their milk intake, and milk sales would plummet. So why wouldn't this assumption apply to cigarette consumption?

The difference is that cigarettes are an inelastic good for consumers. There are no available direct substitutes that provide the same experience, and cigarettes are addictive for users. If you ask a smoker, they will tell you that the addiction creates a need for the consumption of these products. Since this good is inelastic, an increase in price will have relatively little or no effect on the quantity demanded; in fact, demand will remain fairly consistent. Adding a tax (or increasing the price) of cigarettes is virtually the same thing. So how do these additional taxes incentivize consumers to stop smoking and become healthy? The answer is that they don't.

Higher taxes placed on an inelastic good will not entice a significant number of people to stop purchasing the product because of the vast difference in the price of the good. Inelastic goods have a fairly constant demand despite any increases in price.

Here is an economic model to exemplify this claim, followed by an explanation:

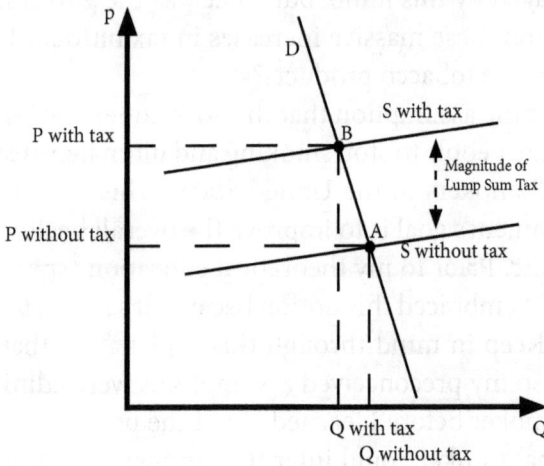

The demand for cigarettes as an inelastic good is denoted by the demand line. Let's start at Point A, the price of the good without a tax. When the tax is applied, the price ultimately increases to Point B. The supply is still the same, so the second supply line is parallel to the first. Because of the inelastic demand, the quantity that is reduced by this tax is extremely small compared to the size of the price increase. The large price increase is passed on to consumers, who will have to pay much more for the same project.

The decrease in the quantity of cigarettes purchased after the imposition of the tax is relatively small compared to the large increase in price. As a rough estimate, the imposed tax increases the price three times the amount that it decreases the number of smokers. Therefore, the consumer pays significantly more for the product, and the number of consumers does not drastically change. The notion that this is to promote a healthier lifestyle is false, so why would the government impose such a burden on the smoking sector of the population?

The answer is simple: tax revenue. Because cigarettes are inelastic, the government greatly benefits from a generous increase in taxes. As just proven, consumers are still willing to purchase cigarettes with little consideration of price changes. The nicotine in cigarettes causes an addiction for consumers of this product; therefore, people crave the product and develop a physical and physiological dependence on it over time. This is a huge advantage and source of revenue for the government. This industry generates billions of dollars each year, so the government benefits greatly from the taxes imposed on those sales. With almost 50 percent of every carton being returned in tax revenues, the government is all too happy to keep people smoking, at least from a financial standpoint.

Since the government is collecting such a significant amount of money, I researched where it this money is being distributed for use. The Center for Disease Control published key statistics related to the use of the revenue from sin taxes. It would be logical to think that the revenues collected from the massive excise taxes would be earmarked for smoking cessation programs and public health facilities to help people quit the habit. In addition, the government could invest the money in preventative measures to educate citizens on the dangers of the product. Unfortunately, only a minute percentage of the money generated from the sales of these products is actually reinvested in the cause.

The Center for Disease Control (CDC) reported that in 2011, it was estimated that states will collect approximately $25.3 billion in revenue from tobacco taxes and legal settlements. However, of that massive amount, only 2 percent will be reinvested in tobacco prevention and cessation programs, a tiny fraction of the revenue generated by cigarette sales. In order to put this into perspective, the CDC reports, "Investing only about 15 percent ($3.7 billion) of the $25.3 billion would fund every state tobacco control program at CDC-recommended levels." Because cigarettes are an inelastic good, the government can count on massive revenue from the product, and the money is then redistributed to pay for other governmental needs.

Most inelastic goods have very similar traits to characterize them in that category. As mentioned previously, there are not a plethora of available substitutes, and the good is a need because it is addictive. This is the reason that demand does not significantly shift on a wide spectrum of prices. A very relevant example of inelasticity is in the pharmaceutical industry.

Why is the Life Span of a Patent Overly Relevant in ec·o·nom·ics?

Prescription drugs are prevalent amongst consumers in the United States for medicinal purposes. In many cases, consumers run a large risk of an injury, chronic pain or illness, or fatality without the medication, creating a genuine need for the product. Because of this, these medications are extraordinarily inelastic. Pharmaceutical patents have been an ongoing issue for this very reason. Let's dig deeper into the logistics of the product and determine how government regulation of the pharmaceutical industry limits consumer usage.

When a patient entrusts their wellbeing to a doctor's care, the orders given are usually followed specifically in order to recover from the illness or injury they incur. Many times, patients are examined and diagnosed with a specific ailment. The doctor then issues a prescription for a specific medication developed to cure the problem. Pharmaceuticals have become so specialized that there are thousands of medicines to treat and cure a wide variety of problems. Because of this, many patients are issued more than one prescription to pinpoint each of the issues with focused treatment to cure or treat their specific ailment or its symptoms.

The specialization of the drugs dramatically inflates the costs for the companies that make them. A multitude of resources, years, and extensive funds are expended on the research and development of these products. Because of this, drug prices can be obnoxiously high.

One of the largest pharmaceutical companies in the world is Pfizer. Among its many products, the company produces a name-brand drug called Lipitor, which helps to reduce cholesterol in a patient's body. The medication plays a vital role in the health of those with high cholesterol problems, and it is essential that these consumers have access to it.

Let's assume a patient is prescribed one dose of this drug each day. The average cost of a daily dose in 2009 was $3.17. This seems like a menial amount of money on a daily basis, but when multiplied by the 365 days in a year, the annual cost of the medication in 2009 was $1,157.05. Even still, a little over a grand for a one-year supply of a medicine that maintains healthy cholesterol does not seem like much. When you look at this from a different perspective, though, it might seem like quite a bit more. Let's look at this from two different viewpoints: a minimum wage earner and an average-median income earner.

The minimum wage in the United States in 2009 was $7.25 per hour. For a full-time employee, the average work year consists of 2,080 hours. Let's assume the employee worked the total hours available (2,080) at minimum wage, making their annual gross income $15,080. If that person was required to take Lipitor at the price of $3.17 per daily dose, the medicine would have cost almost 8 percent of their total pre-tax income. How will they be able to account for the other basic necessities such as food, water, clothing, and shelter? With much difficulty, and that was back in 2009!

The second perspective is from the average-median income wage earner. In 2009, it was reported that the total average-median income was $32,140. At that gross annual income, a Lipitor consumer would be spending almost 4 percent of their income on the crucial medicine. Compared to the minimum wage earner, this actually seems like a bargain, though in reality, it still represents a huge percentage of income spent on just one necessary prescription.

The problem with this example is that it only accounts for a person taking one prescription drug per day. What happens if a minimum wage earner is prescribed two or three drugs? Will they be able to allot 16 or 24 percent of their budget toward prescription drugs and still afford their necessities? The question is not whether they can afford to, but whether they can afford not to. If they can get away with not taking the drug, they are ultimately better off because they will have more money to spend on other necessities. If the medicine is necessary to sustain their health and/or life, they are forced to give up other needs to pay these large sums of money for name-brand pharmaceuticals.

Consumers are paying a premium for these highly specialized drugs. Because of the colossal amount of money spent on the development of these products, the United States government protects the distribution of these drugs by enacting patent laws on branded products. The U.S. pharmaceutical patent laws enable the branded items to remain exclusive in the market for a given number of years.

In other words, even if other companies can mimic the formulations for the products at a cheaper cost, they are restricted from doing so before the life of the patent is over. The average amount of time that branded drugs are on the market before generics can be introduced in the U.S. is between seven and twelve years. This protection is put in place to allow companies like Pfizer to recuperate some of the investment costs in developing the medication. Clearly, these companies—like all companies—are just trying to make money.

Although this seems to be a smart protection for these companies, does this hinder the availability of the products to consumers who don't have enough disposable income to afford their astronomical prices? I stated before that medication is normally an inelastic good; that is, most people need it, and there are few substitutes. The wage earners that were presented would have to allocate a large portion of their income to just one medication. This greatly limits individuals from actually receiving the medicine they need for a healthy living. If they cannot spare additional funds out of their already limited budget, their health will automatically deteriorate unless the medication is not an immediate need. Throughout the lifetime of the patent, the medicine is an inelastic good.

There is one additional option for prescription drugs, and that is to wait. When the seven- to twelve-year patent waiting period is complete, other companies are permitted to create a formulation that is essentially identical to the brand-name drug, one that will offer the same benefits and effects. The generics can be produced at a significantly reduced cost because the pricey research and development expenses are no longer necessary. The formula is required to be published and available from the branded version. As these companies create the drugs, they mass distribute them in all locations where the branded drug is prevalent.

When consumers are given a choice, many will opt for generic drugs. The medication generally provides the same treatment, all while saving the consumers a very noticeable amount of money. Let's revert back to Lipitor for an example of savings. The generic product that came out for Lipitor is called Atorvastatin. The average price of a daily dose of Atorvastatin is fifty-eight cents. Therefore, at one dose daily, it would cost $211.70 annually to pay for a generic prescription to this drug. This represents a discount of nearly 82 percent off the brand name medication for the exact same formulated product. In other words, generic products are significantly more affordable. With such a remarkable discount, it is almost a given that the price-conscious consumer (which most consumers are these days) will choose the generic product. This perfect substitute changes the elasticity of the product, making it much more elastic.

I would like to revisit the dilemma behind these products to delve deeper into what is actually occurring in this process. Typically, the average wage-earning American cannot afford to take prescription drugs because the costs of the medication represent far too high of a percentage of their budget. Is it morally acceptable for patents to protect drugs that are necessities to so many people?

This system forces sick customers to pay inflated rates, limiting some people from having access to the medication based solely on their inability to afford it. If the medicine is an urgent need, the fact that it is vital to their livelihood requires that they designate more of their income to the medicine. On the contrary, should pharmaceutical companies take a massive loss on these drugs just to serve the needs of people? Surely, this is a double-edged sword. It is critical to remember that pharmaceutical companies are exactly that: companies, not charity organizations.

There is not a simple, straightforward solution to this problem. The pharmaceutical companies incur costs in the billions of dollars to develop medications. If they did not pass this cost onto the consumer in the form of inflated prices, the companies would have no reason to be in business. Developing the product does very little for them if they can never recuperate any of the costs associated with research and development; their bottom line would never go from red to black. Ultimately, the development of just one drug could bankrupt a pharmaceutical company, forcing it to close its doors, and no further medications would be developed.

Pharmaceutical companies exist to develop health products and make them available in the market, despite the price. They do not view their products as a moral endeavor to help sick people get better; it is purely business, and they have a product to sell to consumers with the purpose of generating a profit.

At this juncture, it is important to remember that prescription medication is an inelastic good. Despite the price increases, the demand is relatively stable. People need the products to sustain or increase their health status, and pharmaceutical companies are aware of this. If these products were never formulated, there would be a massive decline in health on a global scale. Therefore, it is better that they are in business to develop the medication rather than put out of business for lack of revenue to cover expenses. People will continue to pay a temporary premium for branded products and wait out the patent for generic products. Why? Because they don't have a choice. Economic theory is proof of this.

Chapter Four

Luxury Goods on a Recessionary Budget

Between 2007 and 2008, the U.S. economy went into a deeply rooted recession that changed the dynamics of many markets and industries. Millions of people were laid off or fired and left without the stable income they had relied on so heavily in previous years. Unemployment rates skyrocketed throughout the country.

In January of 2008, the national unemployment rate was 5 percent. By the end of the year, in December, the rate had risen to 7.3 percent. Unfortunately, the rate continued to increase, and by October of 2009, it reached a high of 10.1 percent. These facts are obviously devastating for the majority of Americans that were affected by these changes in the economy.

From the statistics above, it is apparent that the country experienced a difficult economic downturn. I am in no way discounting the hardships that people experienced, but I would like argue that not all effects of the recession were negative. The recession resulted in some positive externalities, though not all are extremely apparent to the naked eye.

How Did Positive Externalities Keep the Economy
Afloat During the Recession?

A positive externality is "an unexpected benefit incurred by a second party that is not involved in the transaction, event, or occurrence." In other words, if one person makes a decision that indirectly influences someone else in a beneficial manner, the second person profits from that decision. There are many instances of these occurring in everyday life.

Let's consider the simplistic example of the homeowner discussed in Chapter 1. If a homeowner makes a decision to invest an additional $5,000 in the landscaping that surrounds his home, he is undoubtedly increasing the value of his own property. When a buyer comes to look at any home in the neighborhood, they will consider the area as a whole and evaluate the value of surrounding properties. Because of this, the neighbors experience a positive externality in the value of their own homes with the landscaping investment. Neighboring properties simultaneously increase in value as a result of the better-looking homes around them.

To dive further into the positive externalities of the recession, let's consider changes in the purchase power of average consumers in the market. People only have a given amount of money in their budget per month. Unless an individual wants to sink themselves into mounds of credit card or loan debt, one can logically only spend as much as they earn. During the recession, the notion of a budget was exceptionally relevant.

For example, if a person earns an annual net income of $40,000, they could theoretically only spend that $40,000. Budgets force people to make choices on purchases. For this example, let's assume that this $40,000 (net income) wage earner designates 70 percent of their budget for necessities; in other words, food, water, clothing, shelter, and medicine (as previously discussed) account for $28,000 of their yearly budget. This leaves a mere $12,000 for additional expenses.

Given the budget above, let's consider a very simple concept to illustrate my point. Most people (men and women alike) who strive to maintain their personal hygiene use a razor on a fairly consistent basis. At any given retail store, an average one-count package of a women's razors is priced at $11.99. The store also sells a four-count refill cartridge for $16.99.

For this example, let's assume an average user goes through one razor per month. For the price of the one-count package plus the four-count refill package, an average woman can invest approximately $28.98 in razors every five months. This use would average out at an average annual cost of about $69.56 per year. If the average woman begins shaving at age fifteen and stops at approximately age seventy-five, the total amount of money spent on razors in a lifetime would be $4,173.60. Although this seems like a relatively low cost per year, the real investment in shaving is the time spent doing it. The average person spends approximately sixty hours per year shaving, a very significant amount of time. The tradeoff of spending this time shaving means that a person cannot be spending those sixty hours working and earning a wage. If a person does not want to invest this many hours a year in this process, they must pay a premium for the alternative to this process.

Laser hair removal is a long-term permanent solution for everyday shaving. This process involves an average of six treatments (usually spaced six to twelve weeks apart) to remove that the majority of hair growth on specific parts of the body. A laser is used to kill the hair follicle each time it regenerates. The process can take an average of six to eighteen months, depending on the area of the body, but the end result is that a person does not have to shave ever again once the process is complete. If the average person spends approximately 60 hours shaving every year for 60 years of their life, this treatment will save them 3,600 hours over the course of their lifetime.

So why doesn't the entire world population get laser hair removal treatments done and dismiss shaving altogether? Because the price of this luxury good is extremely high. A luxury good is "an item that increases more than proportionally as income rises and is not considered a necessity." Laser hair removal is a perfect example of a luxury good, as it is not a necessity, but it provides a significantly more expensive alternative to razors. The luxurious characteristic of the good is the convenience and the amount of time it saves over a lifetime. Usually as people's income rises, they have excess disposable income to invest in procedures like this one.

Let's consider the price of this luxurious treatment process. For a reference point, laser hair removal is usually priced according to the size of the area that is being treated. There are typically three categories of treatment: small, medium, and large areas of the body. A small area consists of the chin, upper lip, and underarms, to give you some idea. Most laser hair removal treatments are purchased in packages of six individual appointments, which are all paid for upfront.

In the Chicago market, the average price of six treatments of one small area of laser hair removal retails for $900. This equates to 21.5 percent of the overall lifetime cost of razors for the average person. Hence, laser hair removal is a luxury good. Most people could not afford to pay $900 per small area to have hair removed, in addition to the cost of hair removal on other parts of the body.

The $40,000 wage earner we talked about earlier would have to designate a specific amount of the $12,000 spending money in their budget. If there is an average of five small areas on a woman's body, this would cost her $4,500 to have just the small areas done, equating to 37.5 percent of the available spending cash and 11.3 percent of the overall annual income. Most people are understandably unwilling to spend this amount of money on a luxury like laser hair removal, especially during a recession, when money is scarce and hard to come by.

Keep in mind that the average person also has many more areas requiring hair removal. The average of large areas, which are considered to be full leg or full arms, is $4,000 per area. Each area accounts for 10 percent of the overall annual budget and 33 percent of the spending money. Most individuals are not willing to pay these premiums when the alternative (disposable razors and personal shaving) is so much cheaper.

However, an increase in income causes people to be more likely to spend money on laser hair removal. The luxury of the good poses an interesting dynamic. There is a vast distinction between the socioeconomic classes that can afford this good, as individuals must have a proportionally large disposable income to afford this luxury. The people who invest their money in this service can simultaneously afford to live in mansions and drive luxurious sports cars.

When the recession hit, businesses had to deliver luxury goods like laser hair removal while keeping the spendable income of the average American in mind. So how did these businesses continue to grow during the recession? Simple! The good ol' Internet. Businesses began marketing their goods and services to the mass public through social collaboration websites that facilitate volume discounts on goods and services.

For example, Groupon launched its website at the end of 2008 during the peak of the economic recession to adhere to what consumers could afford. The website creates daily advertisements of all different types of goods and services for a small fraction of the price they retail for.

The company segments a highlighted deal of the day for users to purchase. The deal is based on the fact that a minimum number of people will commit to purchasing the deal. E-mail messages are sent out to subscribers to directly deliver the available goods for the day. As soon as enough people commit to a purchase each day, the deal is automatically issued to any interested buyer.

The deals are at a minimum 50 percent off of regular price, and sometimes they are discounted even deeper. For example, let's revert back to laser hair removal. The average six-treatment package for a small area on Groupon usually sells for about $150. Reduced from $900, the consumer is able to save 83 percent off the regular retail price. This changes the availability of the product, making it an affordable solution for a larger sect of the consumer base and drastically increases the number of consumers who are able to invest in this luxury good. They will receive the same good for significantly less money.

This is a great opportunity for consumers, but what does this mean for the businesses who participate in these deals? The social collaboration websites are structured to benefit all three parties involved: the consumer, the business, and the website (Groupon, for the sake of our example). The consumer is able to purchase goods for significant price reductions. Luxury goods that they would normally not be willing to pay for became extremely affordable and easily accessible during tough times. The process is also very easy. Consumers can sign up for the city or cities they are interested in shopping in, and they automatically receive a daily e-mail with the deal embedded in it. In other words, the goods come to them without any additional effort.

In one glance, consumers have the ability to decide if they want to make a purchase or not. With one click of the mouse via the Internet or a simple "purchase" button on the Smartphone application, consumers can connect with the goods instantly. The company even allows users to save credit card information so it is literally an instantaneous transaction. It couldn't be any easier for consumers to access these discounted goods.

The businesses involved are also profitable when they participate in such social collaboration websites. The decreased prices offered are at least 50 percent less than regular retail prices. Although businesses may be forfeiting a portion of a higher margin that they normally would earn from a sale, the exposure they receive from participation is vital to the success of the business, particularly during the recession.

One deal can jumpstart interest by thousands of new customers for a company. Once consumers are introduced to a new company and are satisfied with the good they receive, the likelihood of a repeat purchase is exponentially increased. Consumers become company loyal, similar to the way in which consumers are loyal to particular brands. The overarching goal of these companies is to stimulate consumers to repurchase other goods or services that the business offers at regular price, and this enables them to build customer loyalty, an invaluable asset to any company.

The social collaboration websites, Groupon in this example, take a percentage of the sale to cover costs, overhead, and increase profits for the business. In this way, the companies can churn a profit while helping other companies do the same. They deliver top quality products to their customers while building a positive reputation for a newer business model. Groupon has a guaranteed satisfaction for all coupons sold and will refund any purchase that does not live up to a user's expectations. Therefore, they products purchased through Groupon are easy and risk-free. Ultimately, it's a win-win-win situation.

This business model began in November of 2008 during the heart of the recession, and when it took hold, Groupon and other social collaboration websites changed the purchasing power of consumers. As is the nature of a recession, the budgets of most consumers either did not change or decreased. Social collaboration websites used this information to develop a system of consumer purchasing that is beneficial to all parties involved. Therefore, as ironic as it may seem, as a result of the recession, consumers were actually able to purchase luxury items more often than they were in the past. In essence, this shrunk the gap between the socioeconomic classes who stereotypically could or could not purchase the luxury goods prior to the recession.

Groupon also delivers goods tailored to specific customer preferences. The website allows consumers to input some of their personal information to help determine what goods will be of interest to a specific customer. The daily advertisement e-mailed to the consumer is geared to their individual preferences and needs. Not only does this makes shopping on Groupon simple, but it creates a convenience factor that brick-and-mortar stores cannot deliver.

These inputs help the website to cater to the individual directly. Theoretically, if someone is presented with a plethora of goods or services that they are highly interested in, a consumer is more likely to purchase a product. This creates a dynamic customized shopping experience that consumers did not previously have at their disposal.

Social collaboration coupons were only one of the ways consumers changed purchase patterns. Let's consider a second example of increased purchasing power stemming from the recession. As mentioned previously, the massive layoffs left a total of 8.3 million people out of jobs. As people were laid off, jobs were completed eliminated from existence. In other words, companies did not replace the positions with new people. Because of this, there was a massive influx of workers in the labor force and a scarcity of jobs. Consumers were forced to develop other means of meeting their essential needs. More specifically, they found an extreme way to acquire consumer-packaged goods.

For this example, it is important to consider that individuals have a set budget per year, and approximately 70 percent of that is utilized for needs. Let's assume for this example that a couple brings in $60,000 annually and have built a budget based on their combined income. If 70 percent is allocated to needs, that means $42,000 is required to cover needs. Because of the poor economic climate, we will assume that one person was unexpectedly laid off. This person earned $20,000 per year, leaving the new annual household income at $40,000 per year. If $42,000 is needed to cover expenses, how would the couple regain the additional $2,000 shortage?

Many consumers found a new "job" in clipping coupons to save money. This is not a new concept, but it became a trend that has replaced some of the jobs that people have lost. Instead of just presenting a few coupons at the checkout line, people have gone to the extreme. Extreme couponers spent an average of thirty-five hours per week (nearly equal to a forty-hour full-time work week) to save money for their families. The consumers developed shopping hauls that are meticulously planned out to maximize their savings at the register.

A critical part of the planning process is collecting the coupons, and these are generally attained from two primary sources. First, people take the time to print hundreds of coupons from the Internet. Because there are limits on how many can be printed per computer, people use multiple computers to exhaust the greatest number of coupons allowed per household. Coupons are also placed in many local newspapers in various cities. Coupon collectors, therefore, purchase hundreds of newspapers in order to collect the maximum number of coupons possible. This ensures that they are able to save the most money.

Once the coupons are clipped, consumers sift through store circulars and online forums to find where the best sales and deals are on products that coordinate with their coupons. Aside from weekly and monthly promotions, many stores are willing to double and sometimes triple the value of coupons to entice consumers to shop at their outlet. Let's look at how this impacts the actual payout price of the products for consumers.

There are two scenarios that I wish to discuss. First, if a store is running a sale on an item that usually costs $1.99 and is retailing the product for $1.00, the consumer is already saving money for the sale. Consumers pinpoint these sales and find coupons for fifty cents off these products. When these coupons are doubled (per the policy of many different retailers), the products end up being completely free.

There is an additional twist to this deal. If the coupon the consumer has is for seventy-five cents off per item instead of fifty cents, it will still be doubled. This will make each coupon worth $1.50 in savings. If the product is on sale for one dollar, the consumer will net fifty cents back from the store per purchased item. This is important to know because it becomes part of the strategy for people who optimize the use of coupons. This additional money allows couponers to purchase items that they did not have coupons for without spending any out-of-pocket cash. After determining where the best deals are and how to achieve the highest payout on a per-coupon basis, the consumer is ready to actually go to the store.

These individuals purchase cartloads of merchandise to stockpile in their homes. They collected hundreds of items they don't even really need simply because the items are on sale or deeply discounted with coupons, to the point of actually being free or less. So what makes collecting coupons financially worth the time invested in planning and executing the shopping haul? Can a fifty-cent savings per item really add up to be worth the trip? The answer is yes! The return on investment (of time) is exponential. The average savings on one of these trips is approximately 70 to 90 percent off retail prices.

To put this into actual dollar sales, let's say a bill from a huge haul of groceries comes to $1,435.87 retail price. If coupons were applied to this bill with the average savings range, a coupon clipper would expect to actually pay between $430.76 and $143.59. This massive amount of savings equates to thousands of dollars every year, depending on the frequency of trips a consumer takes and the number of coupons and sales they take advantage of.

Consumers literally began using couponing as an outlet to replace the lost job that once plagued their families. At the time, this sounded absolutely ludicrous to me because of my own lackadaisical approach to using coupons. How could coupon use replace an entire salary for a household? The answer lies directly in the numbers.

Let's assume the primary breadwinner in the family remains employed throughout this process. The supplemental income of the person who is laid off is completely deleted from the income matrix. In the example used above, this means the $20,000 secondary income is no longer available and the new annual income is $40,000. In 2009, the average household unit earning approximately $60,000 per year spent a total of $6,372 on food. This means 10.6 percent of overall income went toward food needs.

We've already determined that $42,000 is needed to sustain the same daily life and needs of the household. Therefore, only $2,000 of income expenses is missing from what is absolutely critical for needs. If a consumer was able to reduce expenses by $2,000 or more, it would net an equal payout. In other words, the consumer needs to cut their costs by $2,000, and they will still be equally as happy and satisfied (their economic utility meter would remain stable). With the recession depleting any chance of attaining another job, changing spending habits is really the only logical option.

Approximately $6,372 of the average total expense needs is food. Spending this total amount per year, it would take a consumer about 4.4 extreme shopping trips to the store to reach the average yearly spending on food. The person is, in essence, replacing the time spent at their job in the past with time spent seeking and clipping coupons. Does this pay off?

By using extreme couponing methods to pay for merchandise, the person can expect to actually pay between $1,938.43 and $646.14 out of pocket, depending on the percentage saved. What does this mean in terms of replacing a lost job wage? If the household budgets $42,000 of expenses including an average of $6,372 on food, this means they have an additional $35,628 of expenses to cover.

For the sake of example, let's assume that the coupons equate to only the minimum of a 70 percent savings. This means that instead of paying $6,372 for the year, the person will only spend $1,938.43 for the same amount of food. This leaves the family better off because they gain the difference of what they saved, and they can use that to spend on other necessities. The $4,433.57 variance is additional funds that they can allocate somewhere else or use for incidental groceries and supplies.

Since we determined that they were short $2,000 in their necessary expense budget because of the job loss, let's subtract that from the coupon savings. The household actually ends up with $2,433.57 more expendable income over the previous year because of the savings from coupons. In other words, they substitute coupons as a form of cash, an income source, used to purchase the items they need, and they have a surplus of income left over to cover expenses.

Although consumers were unable to replace the jobs that they lost during the tough economic market, they utilized coupons to acquire the food they needed. The enormous amount of savings of the necessities budget reallocated more funds toward other needs. Because of the budget that was formed prior to being laid off, it is vital that consumers found another way to make up for the lost income. Since jobs were unavailable, couponing became the next best option.

Prior to the recession, only an average of 22 percent of people used coupons. This number skyrocketed to 35 percent during the recession, and it continued to climb to a stunning 37 percent in 2010. This indicates that there is a new standard that people are following as a result of the recession. The impact not only temporarily modified behavior during the rough economic times, but it changed consumer usage patterns permanently.

This was a positive externality because it greatly increased the number of products that manufacturing companies sold. Goods moved through retail faster as consumers gained purchasing power. Consumers are loyal to the brands they desire, and sometimes these brands were the only constant during the tumultuous time. People relied on the normalcy of these stable comfort goods, and they were able to purchase them because of the extreme couponing and promotional activity that occurred during the recession. This process somewhat stabilized people's physiological needs.

The Lipstick Effect

Another stable (and growing) good throughout the recession that women relied on for a touch of normalcy in their lives was lipstick. Although this seems like a relatively generic good, lipstick was an anomaly during the economic crisis of 2008, as well as during the Great Depression in 1929. Lipstick has a simple aesthetic purpose: to adorn a woman's lips and add color to her face. While this seems relatively simple, the cosmetic application of the good is not its only function.

This secondary function of this product was critical to consumer self-confidence during the recession. Lipstick is a good that helps women find confidence in themselves because they feel beautiful when they wear it. With a shortage of monetary funds, stress on adults and their families was at a peak. Consumer confidence was reported to be extremely low during this time because they did not have the purchasing power they once had. Women turned to cheaper goods to gain back some self-assurance and to fulfill the psychological thrill of purchasing goods.

Thus, consumers began purchasing inexpensive luxury goods

such as lipstick. These purchases enabled consumers to replace past goods such as luxury vehicles, outlandish vacations, and costly jewelry while still feeling like they were treating themselves. I'm not arguing that a tube of lipstick replaced a luxury vehicle, but it helped to instill the confidence that one might have gained from larger, more expensive "treats" without cutting into even a fraction of their financial resources. This confidence converted into higher productivity at work and hope for a higher future income as a result. This occurred because of the economic theory known as "the lipstick effect," developed by Leonard Lauder.

The lipstick effect states that when consumers face an economic crisis such as a recession, they will purchase less costly luxury goods to fill the material void. Instead of buying expensive fur coats or luxury shoes, consumers will buy expensive lipstick instead to retain similar effects. Items and services such as lipstick (and other cosmetics), hair products, salons and spas, and manicures/pedicures are substitutes for the guilty pleasures that consumers are used to. They cost significantly less money but still provide the same overall satisfaction.

The difference of guilt in spending between $15 and $20 on expensive lipstick is much less than making an investment in a designer handbag for over $1,000. Consumers are able to still receive the pleasure of spending money on pampering themselves while not committing an overabundance of their already stretched income during a recession.

Similar results occurred in 1929 during the Great Depression, when consumers were fighting to earn money for food. Women would visit the local drug store and purchase bright red lipstick to brighten up their faces. This would increase their perceived happiness and confidence level during what was, by its very definition, a very depressing time. Consumers indulged in small consumption patterns that did not largely hinder their financial status. The products were able to help them to feel satisfied with less than they had previously. Even back in the 1920s, economists argued that having more of something would make a person feel better off. In this case, lipstick sufficed.

Another phenomenon that occurred following the theory of the lipstick effect is coffee consumption. Coffee is one of the most widely consumed commodities in the world. On average, for twenty ounces of a cup of Starbuck's black coffee, consumers could expect to pay around $2.05. This premium price point was higher than many consumers wanted to spend during the recession. Consumers are paying for a top-quality product at Starbucks, not to mention a globally recognized name brand. During the recession, instead of paying this amount, consumers averted to other means to acquire the same product. Realizing that consumers needed a less expensive alternative, McDonald's made a corporate decision to greatly improve their line of coffee products.

McDonald's offered any size coffee, including twenty-ounce cups, for just one dollar. During the recession, consumers were driven by price, and they could save $1.05 per cup of coffee by simply buying it elsewhere. Prices were dictating where people spent money, and McDonald's adapted to this change by promoting their coffee line at a value price.

The new McCafé line of products was also introduced, a high quality of coffee sold for a relatively low cost. Consumers grew accustomed to purchasing a lower cost beverage because the quality was close to equal. This was a good that they were able to enjoy without breaking their bank accounts because McDonald's offered a perfect substitute for Starbucks. Similar to the purchase of lipstick, quality coffee beverages became highly affordable and still delivered the same satisfaction to the consumer that a higher priced latte or cappuccino would.

Skyrocketing lipstick sales were not the only consumer change. As the recession continued through 2008 and into 2009, people began to seek safety for their future. The monthly job losses peaked in January 2009 at 779,000 in one month alone. During this transition, it was vital for people to look for "insurance policies" for the future. I'm not talking about heading up the street to a local State Farm agency; rather, I am referring to a long-term investment in human capital: going back to school.

An overabundance of people was unemployed, and there were not enough jobs for everyone. Unfortunately, the labor force was shifted around. Let me explain what I mean. In a normal economic climate, most jobs require an applicant to have at least a high school diploma. Jobs that require only a high school diploma include (but are not limited to) customer service representatives, cashiers, secretaries, truck drivers, and food service employees, to name a few. These trades require specific skills that an average high school graduate can learn relatively quickly through on-the-job training. On average, these positions usually pay minimum wage or slightly above it.

Prior to the recession, the individuals with only a high school diploma were usually employed in these positions, but this dynamic changed during the recession. Because of the vast influx of available employees in the labor force, highly educated individuals became willing to fill these positions just for the sake of earning a paycheck. For example, many college graduates were not entering the full-time professional workforce directly out of college. The professional positions their degrees had prepared them for were not available because of budget cuts. Thus, these individuals had to take on one or more part-time jobs to earn the money they needed to provide for their needs, and they spent their additional free time looking for positions in their profession.

Instead of these part-time jobs being a temporary source of income, the overqualified college graduates began filling in the gaps of open positions permanently. As a trickle-down effect, this left much of the unskilled labor force jobless. After all, given the choice, why would employers choose to hire an uneducated person if they could acquire a college graduate for the same amount or sometimes less money? You might be wondering why college graduates would be willing to accept such low wages or how employers could possibly pay college graduates less than high school-only diploma earners. Allow me to explain.

Part-time jobs are a perfect solution for a college graduate. A part-time position enables a person to earn a decent amount of money while providing plenty of additional off-duty time to actively interview for a professional career in the individual's field. Without an extremely serious commitment to the part-time position, employers are usually more flexible on shift scheduling with recent grads. In return, they pay a minimal wages (typically minimum wage) for an employee with a premium education.

Sometimes employers are able to pay recent grads less money per hour. Because they leave college without having much work experience, the only base wage that employers can benchmark from is minimum wage. The college graduates are usually willing to accept any wage, as long as they are earning some income to "keep the lights on" while they look for a "real job" in their field. Their primary focus is on the profession ahead of them instead of on the current position. The part-time gig is a means to an end instead of a lifelong commitment.

On the contrary, many of the high school diploma graduates have an average of four years of work experience and the skills that go along with it. If you assume they started working at age eighteen, they will have been accumulating work experience for four years by the time a college student finishes their degree. As a result, these people are able to request a higher salary to compensate them for the skills they have acquired during their work life.

Aside from recent college graduates, high school diploma holders were also competing for positions with people in the labor force who were laid off or fired from full-time professional positions due to the poor economic climate. We can pretty safely assume that many professional positions required at least a four-year bachelor's degree. This literally doubled the amount of (highly educated) people that those high school grads had to compete with. With the decline in employment, landing even a part-time position was an extraordinarily difficult task.

As a result, individuals began going back to school to earn higher degrees to make their credentials more competitive than their peers. Statistically, higher degrees of education result in lower rates of unemployment. In other words, the more education credentials a person holds, the less likely it is that they will be unable to find work.

As a person's educational background increases, so do the percentage of weeks employed on average. In July of 2011, the unemployment rate for people with less than a high school education was 15 percent. For individuals with a high school diploma, the rate dropped to 9.3 percent. The rate dropped slightly once more with some college or an associate's degree at 8.3 percent. Finally, the lowest rate of unemployment fell under bachelor's degrees or higher at 4.3 percent. The percent difference in unemployment from a person with a bachelor's degree versus someone with less than a high school education was an astounding 10.7 percent!

These statistics enticed people of all ages, socioeconomic classes, and education levels to return to school and further their education. Statistically, these numbers indicate that if someone has a higher level of education in their credentials, they are less likely to become unemployed, and this holds true. In fact, the Bureau of Labor statistics has reported that from January of 1992 through January 2011, the proportions of these percentages has remained constant. In other words, as employment rates have increased and decreased through this nineteen-year period, the highest rates of unemployment were always in the category for people with less than a high school diploma.

On the other hand, the lowest rates were always for people with a bachelor's degree or higher. Therefore, this concludes that it is not an isolated measure. On average, the unemployment rate of people with a higher level of education was significantly less even during the recession of 2008 than an individual with less than a high school diploma.

Although people with a bachelor's degree were more likely to be employed, why would someone invest tens of thousands of dollars in education (to earn a bachelor's degree or higher) just to reduce the likelihood of unemployment? There are two more incentives to earn the additional degree.

The first incentive regards the ability of a person to maintain a job for a period of time. Employment stability is much more volatile for people with less education. People with less education lose jobs and rehire more frequently, indicating less steadiness in the market.

As the amount of education increases, the stability is much more regular and levels off. This factor is vital during a recession, when job permanency is extremely important to consumers.

The second incentive to earn a higher degree is in your return on investment. Higher education costs students a large lump sum of money upfront, but the benefits continue to pay off every year in the future. The Bureau of Labor Statistics reports on their website that the more education one had in 2010, the better the median weekly earnings yielded. For example, the average weekly earnings overall in the work force is $782. Someone who has less than a high school diploma makes only 56.7 percent of the average. Those with a professional degree earn 205.8 percent of the average. This is a significant difference.

So, now that the benefits have been illustrated, let's delve deeper into the costs associated with higher education. Even when someone is making $1,610 per week at the professional degree level, how will they pay off an average of $150,000 in school loans to make it profitable for them to have spent so much time in school (the average for a bachelor's and master's degree is eight years)? The $150,000 is based on an average cost of $80,000 for undergraduate degree fees and an additional $70,000 for a graduate degree. If the average person works 52 weeks (2,080 hours) per year, well...let's do the math.

For the sake of this example, all wage earners will retire at the age of sixty-five and will work the maximum number of hours per year without overtime. The average number of working hours in a given year is 2,080. A person who has less than a high school diploma started working at the legal age of eighteen. They will have no debt to pay off regarding school loans or other fees related to education. If their average earnings per week equates to $444, they will earn an average of $1,085,136 in their employed lifetime. This takes into account that even with the extremely volatile unemployment peaks, they would remain employed throughout their available working life.

On the contrary, a person with a professional degree graduates from high school at age eighteen. At an average of eight years to fully earn their education, the age they start a professional position is twenty-six. They must also factor in the debt of $150,000 that will have to be paid back for their education. (For sake of simplicity, this example disregards the cumbersome interest accrued on these large loans, as interest rates would be nearly impossible to factor into the equation for the shear variability in the range of percentages charged.) If the person works the same number of hours per year and retires at the same age as a person with less than a high school diploma, the average lifetime earnings of a person with a professional degree is $3,115,080 after educational debt repayment. This is a 287 percent lifetime increase for an eight-year average investment in human capital. If that isn't a worthwhile payout, I don't know what is!

In addition, the average salary growth per year is much higher for higher levels of education. Not only will higher education consumers start out with a higher salary based on their education, but the increases and annual growth will be significantly more each year. The difference between someone with less than a high school diploma and someone with a bachelor's degree or higher is 3.8 percent in growth each year adjusted for inflation. This proves that there is a very tangible benefit to gaining an education.

Although I am an avid advocate of education, there are a few flaws with the example that are worth noting. First, employees are all paid differently for their hours of work. Hourly employees, for instance, are paid on a variable income ladder. If someone is paid by the hour, they are occasionally given incentives to work overtime. This would enable someone with less than a high school diploma to devote more time to work and earn additional income. Many companies will even pay time-and-a-half or double-time during overtime hours exceeding forty per week. This would skew their average earnings more toward someone with a higher education, as the more time they would be willing to spend working, the more money they could earn in a year's time.

On the other hand, salaried employees are paid on a fixed income ladder. Salaried employees can devote far more than the 2,080 average hours per year to their employer and not be compensated with additional pay. Employees agree to perform a certain amount of work in a year's time for the company at a set amount of pay. Depending on the employee, someone could spend any number of hours performing the job, as long as it was finished. If someone devoted exactly 2,080 annual hours, it would be an equivalent to the number of hours worked to the hourly employee. If an employee is especially efficient and they complete the work in 1,500 hours in a year, that person essentially nets more money on a per-hour basis. They still receive the promised salary but spent significantly less time completing the job. A more lethargic employee might spend 2,500 hours working on the same job during the year. This person ultimately earns less per hour because of the increase in hours worked on the annual basis. The example used does not consider how a person is paid. It is merely an average of all wage earners in the labor force.

Second, to assume that an hourly employee is working the maximum number of hours available is probably not feasible with the fluctuation frequencies of the unemployment rate. The reason for using this number in the example is that it is vital to keep a control number of hours for the example. This is merely an average.

It is also highly unlikely that a person will earn $444 per week every working year of their life. Most of the time, if an employee is working (even during a recession) they expect a raise that is at least consistent with the national inflation rate. The same is consistent with the average wage of a person with a higher education degree. For each year that the person is working, the market prices of goods are increasing at an average rate of 3 percent (the national rate of inflation). If a person does not earn an inflationary raise, they will make less in 2012 than they did in 2011 because the prices of goods will automatically go up. With the exact same dollar income, they have reduced purchasing power.

The example continues to discount the longevity between the different generations of employed people. Let me explain this in more detail. There are a few distinct differences in the characteristics of working people of different generations. The baby boomer cohort tends to make long-term employment commitments with one company for the majority of their career. Millennials expect to have a few different careers and switch employers as often as every one to two years.

The representation of millennials versus baby boomers shows a vast difference in the loyalty they have for the companies they work for. Millennials are twice as likely to leave a company within a year or two. Why is this? As I mentioned in the first part of the book, economists are always looking to be better off, and they respond directly to incentives. So, looking at this from an economic point of view, what factors are enticing each of the generations to respond differently to the employers they work for?

Even after doing hours of research and studying about the trending generational gaps, I did not find the answer to this question until I had dinner with my father, a baby boomer who worked for one company for thirty-three years. Although he had a variety of different assignments within that company, he retired with an unbroken line of service. As a millennial, it was difficult for me to understand why he would remain with one company for such a long period of time. He answered the question with one word: "Pension."

Earning a Pension

Companies offered long-term pensions for employees that would commit to devoting a specific number of years to their organization. Pensions were investments in the employee, and the company promised to pay a specified amount of money for each year of retirement until the employee's death. The employee had to remain employed for a specified number of years and until a certain age. The pension was similar to receiving an annual salary after retirement. The employee could count on a steady income, even during retirement. This is more beneficial than a 401(k) program or a similar financial savings plan because of the sheer size of the investment that the company makes in the employee.

In a 401(k), the employee makes a yearly contribution to basically save a percentage of their pre-tax income each year. The accrual adds up over the years while being invested in a variety of funds. This increases the value of the money. Companies will usually make some sort of negotiated contribution into the fund, depending on how much the employee funds. It is usually a mutual investment, but the financial commitment from the employer is significantly less than that of a pension program.

The difference between a 401(k) and a pension is the amount of money that is contributed by the employer. Pensions are fixed designations of money that is automatically paid to employees, something like a typical salary. In other words, an employee is not required to contribute to a pension because the company pays the entirety of the sum. The downfall with a pension is that the employee is required to stay with one company or risk losing the pension. A 401(k), on the other hand, offers a floating effect because it stays with an employee regardless of what company they work for, even if they switch companies throughout their working life.

For the relation to the example, this might incentivize people to stay employed at a company for a longer period of time, depending on the future compensation packages that are offered. If someone chooses to stay with a company solely to receive the pension, the employee will not have as much room to increase their overall salary on a yearly basis.

Typically, there is a much higher chance of negotiating an increase in salary by moving to another company. If a person decides that it is more important to earn the pension, this could prevent them from significantly increasing their average salary on a yearly basis. In return, they are guaranteed a pension. The averages do not include scrutinized analysis on the effect of this, but it is still vital to recognize that this can influence an employee's decision.

Aside from number of hours worked and retirement benefits, the level of education example also does not take life events, vacations, injuries, or other paid and unpaid absences into account. People's employment does not always directly mesh with their personal lives. Because of this, it is difficult to know exactly what percentage of their lifetime they will actively spend in the workforce. The factual numbers in this example prove that over an entire lifetime of work, the average educated person will earn more than the uneducated individual.

With education proving to be so lucrative for people and market percentages showing an upward trend in the category, why doesn't everyone with less than a high school diploma take the GED (General Education Diploma) test and enroll in college? Mostly, it is because costs are extremely high, and college takes a long-term capital investment. Some people do not have the financial resources to devote directly to education. Also, many people do not want to devote a significant portion of their youth to long nights of studying and stressful test-taking. Even with these hindrances, though, there was a significant increase in the number of people who enrolled.

The massive payouts of education presented greatly incentivized individuals to invest in human capital as their insurance policy during the recession. Without a steady job, the hours of time needed were available to increase the potential earnings for the future. As people learned this, they enrolled in classes and actively sought out higher education. In 2008, the United States Department of Labor predicted that the annual rate of change for education was increasing 2.4 percent; education became one of the fastest-growing commodities because of the significant payouts.

Trends in market needs for skilled labor were also changing. Some of the fastest declining commodities were those that did not require more than a high school education. They included apparel manufacturing (decreasing 7.8 percent), textile mills (decreasing 6.3 percent), hands-on trade industries, and farming, fishing and forestry occupations (decreasing almost 1 percent). Aside from education, other growth areas included management and technical consulting (increasing 6.2 percent) and computer systems design (increasing 3.8 percent). In other words, the growth areas are dependent upon some sort of higher education for a person to even qualify for the position. Even with the credentials, the person has to actually earn the job.

This increase should have resulted in a positive trend line change in the mental capacity of the general public. If the market needs called for someone specializing in management and technical consulting, people would have needed to earn a degree to acquire such a position. Then, they would have been placed in positions that they had studied about and would have been experts in their respective fields. Unfortunately, this picturesque outcome of millions of employed experts is not what actually occurred in the market.

Even with the increase of human capital, there was a negative externality that resulted from this change, as mentioned previously. We previously discussed that many of the jobs that did not require a high school diploma were being filled by recent college graduates. As the recession grew more and more grim and more people enrolled and graduated from college, unskilled labor jobs were being filled with overqualified employees. People with college degrees began serving meals at fast food restaurants, taking any job they could find. This resulted in unemployment for many of those with less than a high school diploma.

This has a cyclical effect on the job market because as more people go back to college (to increase their chances of employment and wage), more overqualified people are dumped into the labor force. The increase in educated people taking jobs for less than high school educated individuals restricts the number of people with less than a high school diploma who can fill the positions. The problem is that there are a limited number of positions available in the entire job market. Even when people go back to school to increase their credentials, there is not a simultaneous increase in the number of jobs in the market.

The negativity that was just presented basically counteracts my argument, but it is important that we analyze these societal trends from both sides of the table. I want to be explicit: My focus is on the positive externalities that stemmed from the changes during the recession, in spite of these mentioned negative outcomes.

The recession presented luxury good seekers, coupon enthusiasts, and education gurus with opportunities and challenges in the respective markets. Throughout all of the negative changes in the economy, there were a plethora of positive prospects for success during the time. The market drastically changed, and people and businesses learned to adapt to "make lemonade out of lemons." In other words, a potentially horrific situation was economically analyzed and altered to match the needs of society. The economic trends varied, but people were able to become "better off," despite the negativity in the market.

Chapter Five

The Theory of Dynamic Inconsistency

The 2008 recession accounted for a variety of changes in the economic market, behavioral patterns of people, and adjustments of businesses. Many of these entities made decisions to adhere to the changes in society instead of attempting to thrive against them. As previously noted, companies like Groupon were formed to cater to the needs of the public and deliver consumable items at an affordable price. It is necessary to consider that "affordable" had a different meaning previous to the economic decline than post (the lipstick effect illustrated this well). As commodities increased dramatically, companies had to develop new methods to deliver high-quality products at a value price.

One of the most successful companies in creating value in the products during the recession was McDonald's Corporation. McDonald's identified an opportunity during the recessionary period (and beyond) to conform to what consumers were looking for. People still needed to feed their families, on a lower income. As a response, McDonald's strived to serve their customers with a value menu full of a variety of low-priced foods. The average cost of an item on McDonald's value menu during this time was around one dollar in most areas of the country.

A customer was able to purchase a McDouble cheeseburger, a small (value-sized) French fry, and a large soft drink for a pre-tax total of three dollars. For the one-dollar price point on each good, it is important to purchase the largest amount one can get from the viewpoint of an economist. More is always better, so a large soda is definitely preferable to a small one, even at the same price point. This was a whole ready-to-eat meal for less than five dollars!

McDonald's reported significant increases in growth during the peak of the recession. In 2005, the company reported in their performance results a 9.2 percent return to shareholders. When the recession began in 2007, McDonald's reported a 20.6 percent return to shareholders and continued to grow in 2009 reporting a 28.2 percent return, almost triple what it had reported just four years earlier in 2005. The significant increase during an economic slump was a direct result of catering to what consumers wanted and—more importantly—to what they could afford.

The three-dollar meal is one example of a value combination that a customer can create. Each item only costs the customer a mere dollar. Even individuals earning minimum wage can afford such a product. The additional benefit is that it has the McDonald's high-quality branded name behind it. Many people cannot re-create a homemade meal consisting of the same products for a cost of only three dollars. It is imperative to consider not only the costs of the raw materials needed to make the food, but also the power used to actually cook it.

For consumers, this seems like a holistic win. McDonald's has approximately 31,000 restaurants worldwide, creating unmatched convenience for its customers. A large majority of these restaurants are open 24 hours per day, 365 days per year. This provides customers with availability at almost any given time. Customers are paying a low price for a good-tasting meal that is affordable even on a minimum wage salary. With all of these perks, what could possibly be a deterrent from customers buying these inexpensive, convenient products?

The answer to this question is not complicated: McDonald's, like the majority of fast food restaurants, offers food that is relatively high in some nutritional content. More specifically, the calorie, fat, and sodium content of the McDouble, value-sized French fry, and large soft drink are a large percentage of the suggested daily intake. Let's digest these numbers a little closer to identify the implications of these nutrition facts in the food.

The published recommended daily intake for adults is an average of between 2,000 and 2,500 calories per day. The graph below summarizes the other average nutritional recommendations that are nationally published:

Nutrient	Unit of Measure	Daily Values
Total Fat	grams (g)	65
Saturated Fat	grams (g)	20
Cholesterol	milligrams (mg)	300
Sodium	milligrams (mg)	2400
Potassium	milligrams (mg)	3500
Total Carbohydrate	grams (g)	300
Fiber	grams (g)	25
Protein	grams (g)	50

Let's use our three-dollar meal to determine the exact nutritional percentages that a person is consuming in this single meal. The first item on the list is a McDouble cheeseburger. A McDouble has 390 calories per serving, 19 grams of fat, and 920 milligrams of sodium. The second item is a small French fry, which contains 230 calories, 11 grams of fat, and 160 milligrams of sodium. The final item for the meal is a large soft drink, which olds 310 calories per serving, 0 grams of fat, and 20 milligrams of sodium. Thus, for the entire meal, a person would consume 930 calories, 30 grams of fat, 1,100 milligrams of sodium, and 148 grams of carbohydrates. This equates to about 46 percent of the suggested daily calorie, fat, and sodium intake, almost half of the daily intake for three of the major categories of nutrition for a person, consumed in only one meal! If someone only ate this meal from McDonald's, they would only be able to have two meals per day without going over the daily recommended values.

Some people do not watch their caloric intake, and others refuse to eat high-calorie foods such as the meal mentioned. For others, outside influences can affect their decision about the meal. Are they running late for an important meeting and have to grab a meal on the go that they can eat from behind the steering wheel? Has a truck driver been driving for six hours without a bite to eat and needs something quick and easy? Is McDonald's the only restaurant open within a forty-mile range or at that hour? Does someone prefer the taste of a McDouble to a Whopper? There is a surplus of contributing factors that can influence one's decision.

How Does Fast Food Intertwine with the Theory of Dynamic Inconsistency?

From an economic point of view, there is an explanation as to why a person would be willing to consume a product at a given time and not another. This economic theory is called "dynamic inconsistency." The theory encompasses the idea that a consumer's preferences change over time, so if a person makes a choice for something one day, they may not choose the same thing at another given time in the future. In other words, consumers have different preferences depending on when they are asked to make the decision.

The most influential factor for decision-making based on this theory is the time implication a consumer faces. In other words, someone will value a decision differently if they are making it for the present or for the future. Even if the decision is for the future, a different value will be placed upon the near future than years or even decades down the road. Let's explore some examples for a clearer explanation of this theory.

First, let's start with the McDonald's three-dollar meal as an example. The consumer is running late for a meeting, and McDonald's three-dollar meal is the only available food item they can purchase and eat within their half-hour of free time. Therefore, their decision is based on a time constraint. This person would be late to the meeting if they went to the next closest restaurant, so this is not an option. The only other alternative is to skip the meal altogether, forcing the person to go hungry for the rest of the day and possibly not perform at their peak during the important meeting.

If a consumer is hungry and they need to make a decision whether or not to eat this high-calorie meal, their hunger is going to inspire the decision they make. A hungry consumer will most likely decide to consume the high-calorie food in the given moment. Their bodily desire is to fill their stomach so that it stops rumbling, and the high-calorie meal will at least fill the empty void. The decision, therefore, is based on needs for the present and not the implications of the future.

As noted above, the three-dollar meal contributes almost half of the daily intake for a person's diet. If a person eats three regular meals per day, they would theoretically be consuming 150 percent of their daily intake. The additional caloric intake typically results in weight gain over a period of time. An additional pound consists of 3,500 extra calories. Because it takes time for the weight gain to occur with small increments of additional calories, most people choose to eat the meal in the present and disregard the future implications involved with selecting a fast food meal.

Another way to look at this is to create meals in the present time for a future period. Let's say the employee headed to the meeting planned out the workday more efficiently that morning. If the person pre-planned their meal, they would still have the choice to consume the McDonald's three-dollar meal or another meal that is prepared in advance. For a meal that is prepared in advance, the person chooses to identify healthier foods with less caloric value. This way, they are able to eat more quantifiable food for a fewer amount of daily calories. Although they are preparing it in the present (before they go to work), they make a conscious choice for the near future (lunchtime during the same day), a choice to consume an amount of calories closer to the daily recommended value.

This is the holistic concept of dynamic inconsistency, but let's take the previous example to another level. What if this same person was on a diet and tried to restrict their intake of calories?

This would make the food choice for the day much more critical. It is much easier for a dieter to make a poor choice for a high-calorie meal one time in the heat of hunger. If someone is especially hungry and must decide what to eat for a current meal while on a diet, they are much more likely to discard the diet. On the other hand, if they are preparing a meal in advance, they are much more likely to choose a healthy meal to remain consistent because they will want to avoid making a spur-of-the-moment decision.

When it comes to this decision, it is important to remember what we learned in the very beginning of this book: Economists are trying to increase their overall utility and always on a quest to be better off. In this example, the present time is critical to consider. If someone is hungry, in the economist's point of view, any available food will make the person better off (or curb the hunger). If the person chooses to forego a meal just because it is considered "unhealthy" by the standards of their chosen diet, they will be worse off in the present time because they will remain uncomfortable in their hunger.

It is much easier for a person on a diet to eat the unhealthy meal in the present and not consider the future implications. If the person actually thought about the weight they would gain in the future from eating the meal, it might incentivize a change in food choice. Theoretically, a person on a diet should be consistent in choosing healthier foods to help them lose weight. Because weight loss is a process that occurs over a significant amount of time, consistency and perseverance is imperative for success. The nature of how to lose weight and the drive of hunger in making food choices are what create the inconsistency.

In addition, it is much easier to start a diet "tomorrow." If someone is not completely devoted to controlling what they eat and following a specific plan, it is much easier to consume a cheeseburger and French fries today and put the dieting off until a "tomorrow" that may never come, for satisfaction is in the present, an immediate result. It is much more feasible to disregard the consequences that will occur in a few months rather than within the next few minutes. The problem is embedded within the desire to satisfy the utility (happiness) of people. If the person upholds the unpredictability by repeatedly starting the diet "tomorrow," they will virtually never actually begin. One would never think the decision-making process in a diet has anything to do with economics, but very simply put, this is dynamic inconsistency.

"I'll Quit Tomorrow"

A second relevant example of this theory is something that was discussed earlier in the book: smoking. It's no secret that cigarette smoke is extremely harmful. A multitude of reliable resources cite the damaging effects smoking can have on the health of tobacco users. According to the United States Center for Disease Control, tobacco causes more deaths annually than all deaths from human immunodeficiency virus (HIV), illegal drug use, alcohol use, motor vehicle injuries, suicides, and murders combined. In addition, smokers die an average of thirteen to fourteen years earlier than nonsmokers. With these statistics backing up the serious ailments of consuming the product, why do so many people continue to smoke?

For one, the product is highly addictive because it contains nicotine. Smokers physically and mentally crave the product regularly. If they deny their body of the substance, they will suffer from withdrawal symptoms. Even when people know that the products are detrimental to their health, it is extremely difficult to ignore the hankering for a tobacco fix.

As a result, most people just have "one more cigarette" to quash present desire. In the same breath, these people vow to quit, claiming it is their "last cigarette" or that they just need this "one final nicotine fix." The reason why I put these words in quotation marks is because most people do not follow these vain promises. Because of the addictive nature of the product, these become routine excuses to take another puff of smoke. This reverts back and directly exemplifies dynamic inconsistency.

Most smokers enjoy the act of smoking. The taste, feel, smell, and overall aura that encompass their environment are things they look forward to. This is also part of the inconsistency. With all of the knowledge of how poor of a choice it is to smoke, people still choose to continue the habit because it increases their utility meter. It is similar to the person who is on a diet. Once a dieter eats food (and once a smoker takes a puff of a cigarette), they instantly perceive themselves to be better off. The gratification they receive from consuming the product (whatever it may be, based on personal desires and needs) cannot be achieved through other means. The smoker is making the choice for "today."

In a given time, the person might strive to quit the smoking habit because they know it is deteriorating their health. It is much more feasible to devote a given time in the future to quit an addictive habit. It literally has no direct influence on the present time other than positively satisfying a strong urge for nicotine.

Similar to the diet example, the negative effects in the future that derive from the present choices are too far off to be perceived as tangible consequences of the action. If someone smokes today, chances are that they will not actually experience any of the negative long-term side effects until years down the road. This is how many smokers justify smoking another cigarette today while promising to quit "tomorrow."

The inconsistency in the decision that a smoker would make between two time periods varies as a factor of when the person will experience the negative effects of the choice. People base their decision-making on when they will experience the repercussions from their choices. Let's use the example of studying for the GMAT (Graduate Management Admissions Test) and then taking the exam.

This exam is necessary for most business students who want to gain admission into graduate school. The standardized test is a measurement of general aptitude with a bachelorette degree. Most graduate-level business schools set the range of acceptable scores according to the school's specific standards of excellence. Once a student takes the exam, the results are sent directly to the schools that the particular student wants to apply for.

I use this example for a very specific reason: The GMAT created a dynamic inconsistency for me and a variety of people that were close to me that took it. A year after I completed my undergraduate degree (during the heat of the recession), I realized that it was imperative for me to build an insurance policy of knowledge for myself. In other words, I decided to pursue my Master's in Business Administration (MBA). The first step in the admissions process was taking the GMAT.

Knowing very little about the actual content of the exam, I trekked to the local bookstore and purchased a 2008 study guide for myself. The guide dissected the exam from every angle. It divulged how the exam was administered, what materials I needed to take with me, how long it would take, and information regarding the scoring process. After the detailed introduction, the guide was comprised of hundreds of practice problems, along with their solutions. I promised myself that I would "study" for two hours every night after work for the next three months. Then, at the end of those well-studied three months, I would tackle the exam.

As you might be able to guess, I found other activities to occupy my time during the designated three month "study" brigade. In actuality, I may have devoted a total of ten hours to some relatively halfhearted problem-solving. I kept telling myself that I would skip studying for the exam "today" (whatever day that happened to be in the fall of 2008) and that I would make up for my procrastination by devoting double the amount of time the next day. I was dynamically inconsistent. No matter when I told myself I was going to set aside time for studying, I always found another activity to occupy my time. This was not going to suffice to earn a stellar score and get admitted to a good school.

After three months passed, I realized that I was spinning on a hamster wheel of knowledge instead of actually learning the material. I was not moving forward. As a result, I changed my plan. There was no accountability for me to study because I didn't have an actual appointment set up to take the exam. My initial plan was to set the appointment after I completed the breadth of studying so I could earn a high score that would get me noticed by the schools of my choice.

Every day, I was living the dynamic inconsistency by claiming I would study "tomorrow." When tomorrow arrived, though, I still didn't actually engage with the material. Similar to the weight loss and smoking, the consequences of my actions were too far out of sight to impact my decision. It was time for me to devise a new plan.

My new plan began with actually paying the $250 fee to set an appointment to take the test. I gave myself two full weeks to study as much as possible before the exam. I now had a vested interest because the $250 fee sank deeper into my pockets than the $28 study guide. After I paid that fee, every day that I put off studying, the pressure only built and the stress only grew. Besides booking the actual appointment, what changed to entice me to increase my study habits during the last two weeks? It was the essence of time.

The consequence of not studying was suddenly much more apparent and timely. I was running out of "tomorrows" and only had thirteen left during the two-week period, at the end of which I would have to go earn my score on the exam. Therefore, the amount of time available for me to devote to preparing for my test was now severely limited. When I was merely studying without an actual set scheduled exam date, I felt like I had an unlimited resource of time. Once I set the date for the test and paid the fee, the time became a much more critical factor in the equation.

With each day that passed, the pressure was more cumbrous because the availability of time lessoned. The time literally became more valuable because there was less of it. Hence, this is the dynamic inconsistency of this example. During the first portion of my studying, diverting study time to another day didn't have as large of an impact as it did once the date was set. When I studied freely without a set appointment, the consequences of not studying (getting a poor score) were too far in the future for me to really care. By adding the time factor to the overall equation, the dynamic inconsistency was integrated.

Why is Today More Valuable than Tomorrow?

Another very relevant example is vacation time offered by companies for their employees. Let's assume that all employees who work for Company X receive ten total vacation days per year as part of their benefits package. The company also has a policy that if a salaried employee works overtime, they can convert the addition hours worked into paid vacation days. In other words, instead of paying an hourly wage for the extra time that the employee spends working, the compensation is made through paid time off.

To make this example simple, let's say an employee works twelve hours in one week over the normal forty hours per week that is required in their contract. This would equate to an additional one and a half days of vacation to compensate them for the time. Company X decides to offer the employee a deal for the extra time they earned. The employee can either take the one and a half days off this year or wait until the following year to use it. If the employee chooses to wait, the company will donate an additional half-day, amounting to two full days of vacation. The incentive "today" is for the employee to wait.

The choice depends on the employee and what the time off will mean for their individual situation. If the employee is overworked and burned out from working twelve hours of overtime (sixty-two hours in one week), the additional half-day offering might not be worth the physical and mental exhaustion. The employee might actually need to rest to recover from the extra hours worked. If they wait until the following year to take advantage of the additional half-day, the additional rest they could accrue from the days off might not be as critical. The value of the time off is different, depending on the timeframe.

In addition, if there are other factors influencing the person's life at the time, the time off might also be more critical. If the employee has a personal matter to tend to that requires time off, it might behoove them to take the time in the present. Let's use a dental visit as an example. Many dentist offices only have availability for patients during normal business hours. If an employee has a toothache or needs a filling, the present value of the time will be exponentially more valuable than the future value because there is some urgency involved to have the dental problem taken care of; the employee likely cannot put it off for a year just to earn another half-day of vacation.

The consideration of these factors presents a dynamic inconsistency in the value of vacation time. The decision that someone will make "today" will differ from the decision they might potentially make in the future because of the contributing factors in their life. What might be a detriment to waiting for the future to take the time off? The necessity of additional time off in the future is unclear.

It is difficult to know if an employee will even want or need the time off in the future. What happens with the time if the employee gets laid off, fired, or quits the position before the vacation days are taken? These scenarios make vacation time obsolete. The employee might not be compensated for the time. The employee would not only lose the additional half-day that was offered but also the twelve hours of overtime compensation that was actually worked. In this situation, it would drastically benefit the employee to take the time immediately for fear of losing that opportunity in the future.

In a different scenario, what if the person is forced to work overtime in the next year without any possibility of using the accrued time? Let's assume Company X lays off 50 percent of its workers, and the remaining employees are assigned double the amount of work. When the employee is told they have to work a certain amount of hours to finish the extra load, the available time to use vacation might become extinct. In other words, the additional demand for man-hours makes it impossible for the employee to be approved to take their vacation. There are a multitude of factors that influence whether the additional time can actually be taken. This must be considered in the present time period, but unfortunately, it cannot be accurately predicted.

Another negative possibility of waiting for the time and gaining the additional half-day is the gamble that the manager who approved the extra time has quit, forgotten, or will not uphold their promise in the future. It is much more difficult to keep track of employee vacation days once the initial earning of them has passed. Even if the manager keeps the most meticulous log of time earned, that log could be inadvertently destroyed or misplaced. Once the record of what has been earned is lost, the employee essentially forfeits all of the time they deserve.

The dynamic inconsistency in the vacation time is an example that is relevant to most people. It is much more feasible to decide on vacation in the present time rather than in the future. The further time is extended through the process, the more challenging it is to make the decision on what is best for the individual. In the example presented, some of the deterrents provide enough motivation to take the time in the present instead of in the future. As exemplified above, the possibility to even take the time in the future might be nonexistent.

Although these various situations are extremely different, they all share a similar characteristic: The dynamic inconsistency theory can be applied to each. This provides answers to explain how and why people make decisions based on the function of time. Time plays a much more critical role in choices than some people realize. The theory proves that people do not necessarily make the same decision for themselves during different periods. It is important for people to make decisions based on "today" and the future.

Circumstances influence the decision-making process, and so does the economic utility meter to become better off. It is critical in the theory for a consumer to determine what choice will return the most beneficial outcome for any given situation. Time is the critical piece of the puzzle that molds everything together.

While we must consider time as an integral factor in decision-making, there is another angle to look at this complicated process.

The beginning of this chapter discussed how the recession forced business, the economy, and people to change habits and strategies in order to thrive in the new climate. Adjustments were not only made in the decision-making process described through the dynamic inconsistency theory. People were forced to evaluate their financial situation, stability, and forecasted future to determine the most beneficial way to proceed.

The Housing "Bubble"

One market that suffered from a particularly large downturn during the recession was the housing market. Prior to the recession, lenders became extremely lenient in regard to the qualifications required to be met for someone to receive a housing mortgage. As it became more feasible for an average person to get approved for a home mortgage, the trend to purchase a house became much more popular. People wanted something they could have ownership over, not just a dwelling to reside in, but something that gave them status as a homeowner. A house was viewed as an investment that someone could gain generous returns on in the future.

People made decisions in the present economic climate. More people began applying for loans, and the lenders simplified the process even more. Prior to the housing bubble, home-loan applicants were required to provide documentation of income, assets, savings of liquid cash, credit history, and history of employment. The strict requirement to prove financial liability was critical to the approval process.

During the mid-2000s, global investors became more willing than ever to invest their money in interest-yielding consumer loans. The investments routed back into the market in the form of home loans. This change, along with the influx of people who desired homeownership, liberalized the application process to a crippling point. Almost anyone was able to acquire a home mortgage with one requirement: a credit score.

If you consider what this actually means, almost anyone

can have a credit score. The second a person applies for their first credit card, even a store card with a small available line of credit, they instantly begin sharing data about their financial status with the world. Every transaction, payment, and interest rate is reported to creditors. All it takes to have a credit score is one credit card—from anywhere. To put this into perspective, I opened my first credit card at the age of sixteen. The company I went through advertised a "building of credit" at a young age. The credit company required a parental cosigner to back up the teenage credit line, and my mom agreed to do this. A credit score is as simple as that, and I had my first one before I was even a legal adult.

People who were completely ineligible under normal circumstances were now able to get home mortgage loans. As long as they had a credit score, a person met the criteria to obtain a loan. This caused a boom in the housing market because almost anyone was able to purchase a home. Unfortunately, many of these people lacked the asset backing and stable income to continually support the loans. Without previous experience of the responsibility of a mortgage, applicants did not know the stringency of the financial commitment they were signing themselves up for.

As people attempted to pay for the financial obligations in the months that followed, they realized they did not have the financial resources to support the loans. To accommodate the amount of money that had to be paid, they had to take out additional loans. As the loans accumulated, the average household income remained stagnant and did not increase enough to enable people to keep up with the debt they incurred at the loan signing.

In 2007, the annual median household income in the United States was $52,673. That number decreased by 1.2 percent in 2008 to a median of $52,029. Why? Because people were spending more money but earning less. Accounting for an increase in inflation, the actual purchasing power of consumers decreased even more. This led consumers to continue to overspend and under-earn, forcing them into even deeper debt.

Thus, consumers were unable to repay what they owed on their properties, and many people lost the homes they had purchased. Lenders had no choice to repossess the assets from the owners who were in default, and the value of the homes significantly depleted immediately. Because this was happening all over the nation, to millions of homeowners, there were not enough homebuyers to purchase all of the unpaid properties. This created a negative trickle-down effect for home valuation; as more and more homes were thrown back onto the market when less and less people could afford them, the value of those homes drastically declined.

When people began to anticipate the loss of their homes, they no longer had a vested interest in upkeeping the property, since they were sure they were not going to be living there for long due to inability to maintain timely payment. Therefore, property maintenance was neglected. The doomed homeowners' negative outlook took a toll on the appearance and condition of many homes. The physical appearance of properties deteriorated, and many homes were unkempt simply because people did not care what the places looked like once they were kicked out. They no longer took ownership in the homes because the homes were no longer in their possession. As the number of homes that were being repossessed increased exponentially during the economic fallout, people began disregarding their responsibility of maintaining their properties. Multimillion-dollar homes were trashed and had to be boarded up. By the time lenders took the homes back into their possession, they were not in a saleable condition.

This reaction not only impacted the consumers whose homes were repossessed, but also the surrounding neighbors. The economic climate imposed a negative externality on many of the people in an area because as the value of one property diminished, so did the value of the surrounding properties. As mentioned in the previous example about an investment in landscaping, potential homebuyers do look at surrounding properties to evaluate the worth of a property they are interested in purchasing and the neighborhood in which it is located. If all of the homes in an area are repossessed due to nonpayment, the value of the area as a whole decreases. As a result, the equity that homeowners previously invested into the home is greatly undervalued.

How Does the Endowment Effect Influence the Housing Market During the Recession?

Why did so many people completely abandon the maintenance and upkeep of these houses that they once took so much pride in owning? There is a simple economic theory that explains the thought process behind the disregard for previously owned property, and this theory is known as the "endowment effect."

The endowment effect states that individuals place more value on a good once their property rights to that good have been established. In other words, people place a higher value on objects they own than they do on things owned by others. Because the theory stresses the value behind owned goods, it is vital to consider homeownership upkeep through this lens.

When ownership was removed from the equation, something changed. Consumers no longer cared for the property they had once invested time, money, and effort into. Explained by the endowment effect, as people began losing ownership for their properties, they lost interest and did not bother with upkeep to something that no longer belonged to them. Why? Because the ex-homeowner's financial reputation was no longer tied to the property. Because it did not belong to the homeowners anymore, they deflected their efforts to focus on their next adventure instead of the failing mortgage. As a result, the property conditions significantly depleted. When the people's rights to the property were disbanded, these consumers literally stopped caring for the homes they had hoped to someday permanently own.

In essence, consumers lost the self-pride that accompanies homeownership. When a consumer is unable to pay for something they own and it is taken away as a result, they no longer have the confidence or the prestige associated with ownership, particularly when it comes to home ownership. In fact, the consumer will actually begin to resent the physical property, as it represents a failed attempt at ownership. During the housing bubble, people who had never dreamt of owning a home were able to do so, though on a far more temporary basis than they anticipated. When the privilege was revoked, consumers reacted by letting the property deteriorate, for the homes were rendered worthless to the consumers who had hoped to purchase them. Thus, these previous home mortgage owners experienced the endowment effect.

On the contrary, not everyone fell short on their mortgage during the recession. Coincidentally, the people who maintained their mortgage during this time experienced the endowment effect in a different way; they were privy to a facet of the endowment effect known as the "query theory," created by Eric J. Johnson, Gerald Häubl, and Anat Keinan to help to explain the process behind the endowment effect.

Query theory argues that the difference in the amount a person is willing to pay for a good (a house, in the case of this example) and the amount a person is willing to sell the same house for is not based solely on the development of ownership. The difference with query theory is that it suggests that individuals go through a specific thought process before determining what a good is worth.

The query theory states that there are certain questions that both the homebuyer and home seller will contemplate before actually putting a number on the table. For the sake of exploring this further, we can assume the most critical questions for both parties to consider are:

> "What are the benefits of purchasing this home?"
> &
> "What are the detriments to purchasing this home?"

The difference between the two parties is the order in which they consider these two questions. The theory states that a seller will focus primarily on the positive outcomes or benefits to purchasing the home. This is because a seller is motivated to sell the home to another person. They want to consider all the positive attributes so that they can convey those to the customer. The consideration of the negative aspects is a realistic consideration, but it is a secondary focus.

On the contrary, the theory also states that the buyer tends to focus on the detriments to the home first. This is because they will be financially responsible for the purchase and the problems that accompany it. Buyers have an incentive to focus on the negatives because this will help to drive down the price that they will be willing to pay for the home. The secondary focus is the positive attributes of the home. This is because this equates to additional conceptual value that they plan to add to the home.

The fact that these questions are processed serially is an important consideration for this theory. This is because experiments show that consumers hold a deeper consideration for the first question that they identify from both standpoints. This means that the answer to the first question is most influential in their decision-making process.

Because sellers focus on the positive attributes of purchasing the home, this ultimately drives up the value, at least in their perspective. They will list the home for a higher selling price than its true market value. This is exactly the opposite for the buyer. Buyers focus on the negatives or perceived flaws in order to drive the value of the home down. This difference is the gap between what the buyer is willing to offer and what the seller is willing to let the property go for.

During the recession, the individuals who retained the ownership over their homes took better care of their properties to increase the value. Their property was a direct representation of who they were, and because of this, these individuals were inclined to preserve it to the fullest. It was critical to retain any value that the consumer had earned in the property to that point.

This would help to uphold the value of the property when and if they ever decided to sell it.

These homeowners had to overcompensate to upkeep the value of their property because their homes were nestled amongst those that had already been repossessed. With query theory in mind, from a buyer's perspective, this was the only way to convey a higher value of a home. Not only were they fighting to retain the value of their home in a normal sense, but they also had to build the equity in the home so that they could continue to attract interested buyers. Homeowners invested hours of their time and much of their money to make repairs and solve problems with the houses; they really had no other choice.

The overall value of neighborhoods began to decline, making it more difficult for people to sell their homes. Let's explore a generic example. A subdivision contains fifty homes, and the average value of each home is $250,000. Four of the homes in the subdivision have been repossessed due to defaulted loans. When the lenders repossessed the homes, the homes were put back on the market for buyers, listed at $125,000 each to recap the lenders' investments—exactly half of the value of all of the other houses in the neighborhood. The decline in value of these four homes has two direct effects on the overall market within the subdivision.

First, the overall average of the homes in the subdivision drops. Instead of $250,000, the average of the homes decreases to $240,000. In other words, even if a person works to increase the value of their home, many homebuyers identify with the average comparisons in the area. People will consider comps in the neighborhood when they want to evaluate what a property is worth in that neighborhood. The negative externality that occurs because of the flipped mortgages decreases the value of every other house in the neighborhood by $10,000.

From a homebuyer's point of view, they would be paying too much by making an offer for even a penny over $240,000. On the contrary, the seller who invests thousands of dollars to increase the value believes that this offer will significantly undervalue their property. This causes a direct disconnect between the parties, buyer and seller.

The second effect that occurs is the significant decline in the likelihood that a house listed at $250,000 will sell. Price is a huge factor when a buyer is considering purchasing a home, perhaps the most expensive one-item purchase they will make in their lifetime. If every home in a neighborhood is valued at $250,000, each has the same probability of selling based on price alone. When houses are resold after repossession, however, they are typically listed for significantly less than the value of the initial mortgage in order for the lender to try and acquire some of the loss from the upside-down mortgage.

Buyers expect the full-value home sellers to be competitive with the other homes in the neighborhood. In this example, the four homes were listed for $125,000. In a price-conscious market, most homebuyers will not want to pay $250,000 for a property if there are other comparable homes available in the same neighborhood for half that. This greatly disadvantages the homeowners who actually managed to pay their mortgages because they have less of a chance to sell to buyers. In a nutshell, the attractive price point of the foreclosed homes deters individuals from the more expensive houses.

There is an anomaly in the price of these houses. Even if the homebuyer paid $125,000 for a repossessed home and had to invest $30,000 to renovate the home into move-in condition, the savings on the lower price would still be a net of $95,000 as compared to the other houses in the neighborhood. This is a significant amount of savings for any homebuyer. The only trade-off is that they must invest time fixing the home up to their specifications.

The recession churned out millions of home foreclosures and forced those homes to be made available to new buyers at a reduced cost. This resulted in a massive drop in the number of new houses that were built after the recession. The National Association of Homebuilders reported that in 2005, there were 2,068,300 housing starts available, the beginning excavation and structures of actual ground in place to build residential housing. In other words, there were over 2,000,000 lots available with the potential for new homes. (This term is used as a measurement because not all new home projects are completed for a variety of reasons.) In 2010, however, just 5 years later, only 587,600 housing starts were reported. This represents a 71.6 percent decrease in the number of potential new homes. What changes were made to influence these drastic numbers?

Foreclosure homes were readily available because of the massive number of homes that were repossessed during the recession. As previously mentioned in the example above, foreclosed homes that are put back on the market usually advertise significantly competitive prices to compel buyers to purchase them, as lenders desperately want to recoup some of the profits they lost when the initial mortgage fell through.

Through this process, consumers learned that not everyone fit the homeowner profile. Some mortgage holders could not keep up with extensive payments, and they lost their homes in the process. Dynamic inconsistency played a role in the housing market in this case. In the heat of the trend to take out a mortgage and own a home, it seemed like a practical decision to take a large sum of money. Consumers thought about their current situation and assumed that their salaries would only increase. Unfortunately, instead of the prosperous economy they were hoping for, the nation was hit with a recession.

Let's look at a more simplistic example of the endowment effect through another commodity. Consider used books being sold at a garage or yard sale. When a person purchases the books brand new, they take ownership of them. Let's assume each book originally sold for an average price of twenty dollars. At the time of the initial purchase, the buyer sees twenty dollars' worth of value in the book. After they take the time to read it once, the value of the book ultimately goes down in the eyes of that person. No matter how many times the person rereads the book, it will never have the same initial effect. The value of the "unknown" information in it makes it worth the reader's time, but when everything in the book has already been disclosed, the value of the book and the knowledge or entertainment within it drops significantly. Therefore, the person decides to sell that book and all others that they already read in the garage sale.

Garage sales have a history of hosting exceptionally cheap deals on items that are still quite useable. Unlike some items, books have a higher value for each new reader. In the garage sale for this example, the owner prices the used books at five dollars each, which is 75 percent off of the original retail price. When a seller comes up and shuffles through the multitude of books in a pile, the seller bargains and makes an offer of five dollars for four of the books.

This might seem drastically low, but it is a very realistic offer. Garage sale shoppers are looking for extreme deals and will attempt to haggle with the seller. These sales are usually grouped together with multiple venues in a specific geography. Not only does this help to lure buyers into the area, but it also facilitates an easy transition from one place to the other. Because of this, sellers need to be flexible on the prices they charge. If they aren't, buyers will migrate to other sales in the neighborhood to find a better price.

There is one issue with the flexibility of sellers. Because of the endowment effect, sellers take ownership over their belongings. They try to ask for too much money in the present for items that they once valued at a much higher price. When the buyer in the example offered a significantly lower price for the books for sale, the theory claims that the seller would react poorly and almost become offended by the low offer. The seller would not accept the lower price because the conceptual value of the books is higher simply because the person owns them. In the endowment effect, the pride of the ownership holds value for the seller above and beyond the actual cost of the good. This can have negative effects when sellers hoard useless items based on an emotional attachment.

A similar outcome occurred in the housing market, albeit with a slightly different twist to the economic theory. Homeowners were unwilling to sell their properties for any less than what they believed their property was worth. As the number of foreclosed homes increased, the value of homes around the foreclosures decreased as a result.

The economy worsened, and the increased supply of homes in the market was not matched by an increased demand. Instead, people upheld the pre-recession high-priced values of their homes. Because of the endowment effect, the ownership of their homes drove them to charge above market demand and average prices.

Purchasing a larger home was deemed by most people to be luxurious, so the decision made in the present was practical. However, the changes in the recession changed that thought process. People began taking the financial incentive of the repossessed homes that were offered or renting from a landlord. The decisions made prior to the recession were not the same as the housing choices made after the recession. This was a case of dynamic inconsistency. Consumers began realizing that it was more fiscally stable to purchase below what they could actually afford. This would leave a "cushion" of additional income in case of financial loss.

Of course the recession changed the economy drastically. People had a financial incentive to eat fast food at only three dollars per meal. Students had an incentive to wait to study until right before they took a test. Consumers who were thinking about starting a diet had very little incentive to actually follow through with the diet, even from the first day. People took out subprime mortgages that were far beyond their financial means of feasibility. All of these examples could be explained through the theory of dynamic inconsistency.

The choices consumers made reflected their decision-making process based on the present. If someone smokes a cigarette today, the chances of them feeling any effects of it tomorrow (or any day relatively soon) is highly unlikely. It is all part of the decision-making process based solely on when the consumer will experience the consequences of their decision. Sometimes it's not as simple to think "today's" decisions through to the consequences of the future.

Chapter Six

Why Is It Profitable to Scalp Football Tickets on Game Day?

Consider the meaning of the old adage, "One man's junk is another man's treasure." The concept here encompasses the idea that even if a good is not valuable to one person, another individual might find a significant worth in it. In economics, the value of a good is intrinsically determined by what a consumer is willing to pay for it. Although prices are usually "set" by the supplier of the good, consumer demand drives the ability of the supplier to determine what that price will be. If consumers are not willing to pay the set price, it will have to be lowered.

The economy is completely variable. The fluidity of the constantly changing prices reflects the change in supply and demand. Theoretically, if there is a massive influx in the market supply of widgets without a consistent matching increase in demand, the price of widgets should drop. On the contrary, if there is a massive increase in the demand of widgets without a matching supply increase, the price should drastically proliferate. This is not always the case however. In reality, there are not a set numbers of goods produced to match a set number of goods demanded.

Depending on the good, there are a variety of changes in supply, demand, and the price that influence production and consumption in the market. Some goods are produced with a maximum cap on the total. The limited availability of these goods changes the demand structure. Other goods are only produced seasonally, and some goods are inferior to their substitutes. Truly, the value is in the eye of the consumer.

The prices of goods change depending upon inflationary increases. Inflation can be defined as "an ongoing rise in the general level of prices in the economy for a relatively similar good over time." In other words, the value of one dollar today is less than the value of the same dollar in the future. This theory assumes that there are no major improvements on the product to warrant a significant increase in price. For the entire United States, this is measured annually. The average inflationary increase in the United States is approximately 3 percent.

Inflation is an economic explanation for changes that naturally occur in the market. It is a measure of the purchasing power that consumers have over time with the same money. Since 3 percent inflation is the national rate, this means that one dollar in the present equates to only ninety-seven cents of purchasing power in the future. This does not mean that a physical dollar from one year can only be exchanged for ninety-seven cents the next year. Rather, it designates that a good that could be purchased with $1.00 one year will actually cost a consumer $1.03 the following year.

Inflation has a direct influence on a plethora of goods in the market. Although inflation occurs on a national level that affects the entire market, specific niches are more drastically impacted.

Let's revisit the example of the football game from the beginning of this book. Before taking your seat and ordering your favorite cold beverage at the football stadium, you had to purchase tickets to the game. There are two main mediums to purchase tickets: the actual ticket venue at the stadium or a third party that resells the tickets after market. The majority of sporting event tickets is sold to the general public through a third-party sale.

For this example, we will assume that you purchased the tickets from a season ticket holder who owns the rights to the seats. The face value of the tickets that you purchased is sixty-eight dollars each. Let's assume the season ticket holder charged you $150 per ticket. Obviously since you were able to order the beer at the game, you paid the $150 price per ticket that the supplier of the tickets required. This means that you paid 2.2 times the face value of the ticket. Why was the price of these tickets so incredibly inflated? Did the cost of tickets in general increase faster than the overall national inflation rate of the entire market? The answer is no.

Some goods such as tickets sold by a third party are temporarily inflated. There are a few causes to create this anomaly. First, there are a fixed number of seats in the stadium. As more seats sell out, the ones that have not sold become more valuable. In other words, the demand remains constant as the number of tickets depletes. This drastically inflates all of the other tickets that are resold through a third party.

Second, prices for tickets tend to inflate or deflate throughout the season, depending on the quality of the team and the specific opponent they are playing. As teams win more games throughout the season, tickets to the games become more expensive. If a team is better, more people will follow them. In addition, if an opponent has a winning record, the game tickets are usually inflated because fans will anticipate it to be a more exciting game.

A third reason for the inflation is that people use resale of tickets as a form of income. Many ticket brokers buy large quantities of tickets for football games and resell them to fans later in the season. If fans only purchase one set of tickets for a single game at a time, they are usually willing to pay more. This enables ticket brokers to charge a higher price for individual games. As an incentive, many ticket brokers will offer volume discounts to fans who are looking to buy more tickets.

These three explanations have an overarching trend between them. The resale value of goods is a direct function of demand in the market. As the demand of a good (the ticket, in this case) increases because of the reasons presented above, the resale price simultaneously increases. Consumers are demanding a good that has a maximum cap of production in a given period of time. Even if 1,000,000 fans were willing to purchase tickets to a game, there are still only enough tickets as there are seats in the stadium, thus limiting the number of tickets sold.

This type of inflation did not stem from an actual change in the market. Instead, the ticket prices were only temporarily inflated as a function of the demand for the product. When more people wanted to attend the football game, third-party sellers used the opportunity to increase the price. Individuals in this example compete with one another for the chance to purchase tickets. The more money an individual is willing to offer, the higher the likelihood that they will "win" the opportunity to buy tickets. The key to this concept is the fixed number of tickets.

The secondhand market of resale goods proposes some a variety of applicable price fluctuations besides the inflated event ticket market. Resale goods can also provide consumers with a deal for a higher-valued item at a lower cost. For example, an airline voucher for a free flight might be administered to someone who gives up their seat on an overbooked flight. If the recipient of the free flight does not see a use for it in the future, they have the ability to choose to sell the certificate.

For this example, assume that the average round-trip flight is approximately $250. The voucher is applicable for any flight that is advertised to cost $250. The voucher clearly states that there is no cash value for its exchange. Because of this, the owner of the certificate has a strong incentive to sell the voucher for less than the proposed $250 value. Let's explore this concept further.

The owner of the voucher decides that any form of cash will make them better off than the voucher they already have. The piece of paper that has a $250 value equated with it is literally worth nothing to the recipient without the need of another flight. The owner of the voucher can choose to resell the voucher to another individual who can use it at a lower cost than the flight value of the certificate.

For example, if the voucher owner sells the certificate to another person for $150, it is mutually beneficial for both parties. In addition, there are positive externalities from the transaction. The owner of the voucher has now liquidated a useless flight voucher for $150 cash instead of wasting both time (for the flight that was given up initially) and money. The recipient of the purchase will be able to fly for $100 less than the regular price of the flight.

The airline also benefits from positive externalities for a few reasons. First, the airline was able to fill the initial airplane with the correct number of scheduled passengers. They were able to issue the voucher to a passenger who was willing to wait for another departure time to compensate the customer for the new flight. This kept all passengers satisfied.

Second, the incremental cost of one additional passenger for a free flight (through the use of the voucher) is relatively miniscule. An airplane is scheduled to leave Point A and arrive at Point B months before the airplane actually takes off. The costs to send the airplane on that voyage are fixed and do not significantly increase depending on how full the flight is.

Flights are measured with a break-even point. There are a specific number of passengers that pay enough money to cover the costs of the flight. If more passengers beyond the break-even point purchase tickets for the flight, the flight will generate a higher profit. Adding one additional passenger for free does not change the profitability of the flight, as long as there are enough full-priced passengers onboard.

If the passenger ends up liking the airline, they may become brand loyal. This would benefit the airline because it is such a competitive industry. If a passenger continues to fly the same airline in the future, the airline will enjoy continual business and possibly positive word-of-mouth advertising. With a large enough clientele base, this could theoretically reduce costs on advertising because they will already have brand loyal consumers. The airline can forego some advertising costs that would have been spent on enticing consumers. It will also help to ensure that passengers will be traveling on that airline in the future.

In this example, the resale of the ticket voucher is undoubtedly a function of demand. There is a high demand for air travel but very few ways to earn reduced rates. By taking advantage of a resale for a voucher, the buyer and seller are able to benefit.

The demand function for resale definitely dictates the price that a good will resell for. The economic theory of demand assumes that when consumers find a need for a good, demand increases. As noted in the football ticket example, a defining characteristic of resale goods is that there is usually a fixed number of goods produced within a given time period.

This assumption is prefaced on the idea that newer or improved goods (even if they are very similar) are still superior to used goods that are being resold. The incentive for a consumer to purchase a used good via resale is the value of a cheaper cost for an item that is still functional. A very popular and lucrative resale market for functionality of goods is in educational textbooks.

An Exemplary Model of Profitability: The Textbook Example

Chapter 3 discussed the fundamental necessity of a strong educational background for a secure future. The data pulled from the national average salaries of individuals with education credentials was almost three times over a working lifetime than that of someone with less than a high school diploma. Unfortunately, one of the tradeoffs to earning a degree is the large upfront investment costs required to pay for school.

One of the most significant costs, aside from tuition, is textbooks, which cost students massive sums of money every semester. In 2010, the College Board reported that the average cost of textbooks for one undergraduate school year was $1,137 at public colleges and $1,181 at private colleges. This equates to a four-year total of $4,548 for public college and $4,724 for private college students.

A choice students face is whether to purchase new or used textbooks. There are financial benefits for both, depending on the individual student's needs. The resale involved with used textbooks has massive profit potential if someone sells large quantities. The only stipulation in this resale process is that the demand for used books depends on the textbook requirements for the classes that students take. If no students enroll in a class that had a ton of students the previous semester, there will be an overabundance of used books with no demand for them.

Students have a choice whether to purchase books brand new. If they do this, they will inevitably end up paying a higher price. There are some advantages to this though. Because some students take notes and highlight text directly in their books, it may be a relief to know that brand new copies will be completely free and clear of writing or highlighting. A second advantage is that brand new books are more readily available because they do not have a fixed number that is produced. New books also have the most current information if they are updated.

Students can also elect to purchase used books. The resale of the goods is beneficial to students because the price is usually significantly less than new books. Used books are functional items that can still be applicable for the classes a student is taking. However, students run the risk of purchasing the wrong edition of the book, perhaps an outdated one. In addition, pages may be ripped, marks might be made on the pages, and the quality will not match a brand new textbook. There is also the possibility that a used book will not be available if no one purchased it in the past.

Used books that are recycled and resold from year to year are generated from students who complete a specific course and do not need the textbook anymore. Bookstores will offer a certain amount of money for the books that students sell back. The percentage of cost offered depends on the demand for the book or number of students who usually take the course corresponding to the book.

The refund is also a direct function of current inventory needs. Bookstores will determine how many of each textbook they think they can sell during the next semester of classes. For example, for Math 101, a bookstore needs thirty used textbooks for the upcoming semester. If the bookstore has already paid thirty students for their books and the thirty-first student tries to sell theirs back, they will probably either be denied an offer or given a marginally low offer. This system allows students to earn money back on used books while simultaneously allowing the bookstore to offer the next round of students a cheaper alternative to brand new books.

In order to truly exemplify how this works, let's use textbook purchase trends gathered by a public university. The University of North Carolina performed a study with fundamental data to explore the resale value of textbooks. The data was collected from all of the satellite schools and the main campus, which make up the school network. During the 2009-10 school year, the average student paid $616.76 for new textbooks. This is almost half of the national average. On the contrary, the average student paid $466.74 for used books. This means that on average, students are saving 24.3 percent just by purchasing used books. This is a significant amount of savings, especially when calculated over a four-year college career.

A second factor to consider besides saving money is the average percentage of money that selling books back can return for students. This number is critical because this factors the net amount of money that a student can expect from buying and selling back their textbooks. New textbooks yielded an average of $94.19 back for resale at the end of a semester. Therefore, students received an average of 15.3 percent of their money back on what they originally spent.

On the other hand, used textbooks yielded an average of $68.77 at the end of the semester. This is an average of 14.7 percent of money back. As a result, there is not a significant difference in the actual percentage of money that both types of books return to students. This indicates that textbooks can be resold multiple times.

In the 2006-07 school year, an average of 76 percent of students purchased new textbooks, while only 24 percent of students purchased all used textbooks. Beginning with the recession through 2010, these numbers have drastically changed. The data on textbooks demonstrates that more students now purchase used textbooks instead of new ones. There was an 8 percent shift in the number of students between new and used textbook purchases. The significant increase in the used textbook market displays a higher demand from students for a more affordable deal.

The resale prices are approximately 25 percent lower for used textbooks. Sales for these books are still determined directly by the number of students who need them for class. Trends for books have changed drastically, and students have adapted to invest more of the money necessary for college to tuition payments. Although the prices of used textbooks provide a less expensive alternative to brand new books, there is another source for textbooks that usually represents an even more significant savings. This option is the international edition of a textbook.

International editions of books are produced globally in a variety of countries. These textbooks deliver the same information to the consumer while drastically cutting the price. Manufacturers typically alter some of the resources that are used to produce the books to drive the cost down, creating a few differences in the quality and content of the overall books.

For example, international editions are printed on lighter-weight paper to reduce input costs on raw materials. Books are held together with lower-quality bindings. Some of the international editions are only available in paperback, even if the U.S. counterpart comes in hardcover. Many of these books are printed without color plates because the cost of colored ink is marginally higher versus black ink. In addition, many of the manufacturers do not acquire the permission of the U.S.-based publishers who own the printing rights to the book. Each of these production shortcuts are used to eliminate unnecessary up-charges that are passed through to the consumer in the United States.

The presented changes in production are implemented to reduce production costs. This ultimately leads to cheaper books for the consumer. What are the price differentials between the international edition and the U.S. edition of the same book? Are there any other implications besides slight quality differences to purchasing these cheaper items? The actual information delivered within the pages of the book is equal to that of the United States. The cost savings is merely in the physical body of the book itself.

An article in The New York Times Online, published on October 21, 2003, discussed the differences in prices for U.S.-published editions of books versus internationally published ones. The article highlighted two textbooks. For the book Linear System Theory & Design, third edition, the retail price for consumers was $110 per book. For the international copy of the same book, the retail was $41.76. There was an additional charge for shipping and handling of $8.05 per book, which brought the total for the book to $49.81. This means consumers saved a total of $60.19 per book. This equates to the consumer only paying 45.3 percent off the retail price of the U.S. version of the book by actually buying the international copy.

The second book mentioned in the article is Lehninger Principles of Biochemistry, third edition. I wanted to figure the savings for more than one book to prove that a specific publication is not an anomaly among the thousands of textbooks available on the market. The average retail price for a copy of this book produced in the U.S. costs the consumer $146.15. The international edition retails for $71.53, with shipping and handling included. By purchasing this book in the international edition, the consumer saves 51.1 percent of the cost. In both cases, the consumer is paying less than half of the price in the U.S. market.

On the surface, it seems completely ludicrous for anyone to purchase the copy manufactured in the United States for a higher price. The only reason someone would is if they are looking for a better quality of book or hardcover version. Like anything that seems too good to be true, there is one stipulation that influences the purchasing decisions of consumers for international editions. Most commercial resale venues will not pay consumers for the international copy of a book. Therefore, there is little to no resale value in international editions.

In order to determine whether purchasing the international

edition is more financially responsible than the U.S. edition of any book, we have to calculate the net cost for each book. In other words, the net cost of an international edition is what a consumer pays initially because they cannot be resold commercially. For U.S.-based editions, the net cost is actually the original cost spent to purchase the book minus the money that is gained back once the book is sold after the student uses it and sells it back to the bookstore.

When a student is finished with a book at the end of a semester, they have to find a medium to sell their books back. The website BookScouter.com is a holistic tool in which consumers can input the identification code (ISBN) of a specific book, and the website pulls all of the prices that are being offered on the Internet to sell the book back. The website accumulates all of the available offers to help students determine the highest amount of money they can receive back on their textbooks. In order to continue the example above, I entered Linear System Theory & Design, third edition, into the website.

The range of offers for this book varies from the highest cash offer of $44.00, all the way down to $14.48. The willingness of the companies on the Internet to purchase these books back from students is completely dependent on the demand for the book and the current stock of inventory. As demand increases, the amount that students can receive increases, as long as the inventory is not too high. Let's assume that the student who is reselling the textbook is an economist and always wants to be better off. The best choice would appear to be accepting the forty-four dollars from the website that is making the offer.

Since the original price paid for this book totaled $110, we now need to subtract the money that they will receive from the resell of the book, for a total of $66. The total net price of the international edition is $44.81. Even without being able to sell the international edition back, the consumer is still saving 32.1 percent by purchasing the global copy of the book. This is a massive amount of savings.

The second book, Lehninger Principles of Biochemistry,

third edition retailed originally for \$146.15. The ranges of offers posted on BookScouter.com were surprising. None of the vendors online were willing to pay even one cent to purchase this book back. Therefore, the consumer is stuck paying a net of \$146.15 for the book. The international edition is a much better option in this case, since it retails for only \$71.53.

There is a problem with the United States publishing practices when it comes to resale of books. Many authors will issue new editions of books frequently. They have the ability to change any of the information in the book at a given time. Even if the author alters only one single word or a sentence, it is consider a completely new edition. In our example, when the "fourth edition" is created, it renders the third edition null and void. Therefore, companies are unwilling to pay a significant amount for the recently outdated copy of the book.

In the case of textbooks, many authors are professors who write the copy for the classes they teach. Approximately once per year, the professor will issue a new edition of the book, which they will use as the required course material for their classes. This forces many copies of the textbook to be sold.

There is an anomaly with this situation. Professors who author books do not make any money on the resold copies of the book. By frequently creating new editions, professors eliminate the number of copies that are resold and generate personal revenue through book sales. The higher the number of newer editions sold, the larger amount of money they will make. As stated above, changing a textbook only requires a minimal difference between editions. This creates a large incentive for professors to publish books and develop new editions frequently.

The differences in price for books reflect the demand structure for the specific copies of the book. The price can vary greatly if a consumer is willing to substitute the physical form of the book for a lower-quality one produced internationally. As the demand for books increases, the price adjusts accordingly. The resale value of these goods is a direct function of demand. Not all resale goods are a function of the demand like textbooks.

Some have distinct characteristics that alter the demand and timeliness of the resale. For example, let's consider used jewelry that is put on the market for resale.

After a couple has been dating and they want to make a stronger commitment in the relationship, most men begin hunting for the perfect engagement ring. Men spend hundreds or even thousands of dollars on this token of their affection. The value of the ring far outweighs the dollar value that is associated with it, for it is a token of love and devotion to remain with the person forever. This is the theory of engagement.

Men spend time to plan the perfect setting to propose. Usually, when a man kneels down in a romantic setting, most women know that their Prince Charming is about to pop the question. If the relationship is steady and she gleefully accepts, both members of the couple celebrate with their friends and family. The couple then spends the entire length of their engagement planning the ceremony and celebration of their lifetime for the big day.

On the actual day of the wedding, the couple makes a promise of forever and vows to share a lifetime of happiness with one another. Unfortunately, this is not always what the actual outcome of the marriage is. The United States CDC reported that in 2009, the marriage rate was 6.8 percent. Although this is a high number, the divorce rate is exactly half of that, reported at 3.4 percent. That means that on average, half of all marital relationships end in divorce.

The year 2009 was not an unrealistic year for a spike in divorce rates. In 2007 and 2008, the divorce rates were noted at 3.6 and 3.5 percent, respectively, which accounted for approximately 50 percent of all total marriages. Don't get me wrong, as I am not opposed to marriage and believe in the institution of it wholeheartedly. I am merely using as an example to explain the resale of jewelry.

When a marriage fails, there is a plethora of negative emotions associated with the entire situation. Two people who were once in love, devoting their lives to each other, decide to separate, which will change their lives significantly. Generally speaking, the largest physical token involved in this process is the gift given during the proposal: a diamond ring.

The ring is a physical symbol of the emotional feelings held between two people. If an engagement or marriage crumbles, most people want to dismiss the physical representation of the joint venture, since the ring is a painful reminder of a broken connection and a broken heart. Therefore, there is both a financial and an emotional incentive to sell the used ring. In this sense, resale of the good is not solely for financial gains.

The demand for a piece of jewelry such as a used engagement ring is extremely variable. There isn't a consistent timeline for people to get engaged with one another. In addition, many people do not purchase used jewelry when they are getting engaged because of the availability. Most of the time, the only used jewelry that is available comes from people who break off engagements or marriages or perhaps from estates of those who have passed. The number of breakups varies greatly during all periods of time that can be measured.

A person who has just experienced a serious breakup usually wants to get rid of any reminders of the relationship as soon as possible, including the engagement ring. This creates a higher incentive for the seller to find a buyer than the buyer has to find the good. Because of the lower (and extremely variable) demand for an expensive piece of jewelry, the resale value of engagement rings is typically far less than the original selling price. The retail diamond market also affects how much money a seller will receive for their used jewelry. The price and value of diamonds is extremely volatile.

Let's consider the price of the diamond engagement ring when it was given to the person who is now trying to sell it. If the couple got engaged in May of 2008 and sadly ended their engagement in November of 2009, the value of the diamond ring drastically changed. For the sake of simplicity, let's assume the diamond weight was four carats. Because of the volatility of when the couple purchased and tried to sell the ring, they could expect to pay a difference of approximately 26 percent total.

Even though this person will be losing a significant amount of money by reselling the ring for far less than it was originally purchased for, the emotional burden that the ring represents will be dismissed with the sale. This is beneficial for the seller for two reasons.

First, there will be financial incentive for the seller to give up the ring. The woman will ultimately make a profit by liquidating some of her assets. The second and larger enticement is that any harsh feelings or sentimentalities tied to the ring need to be removed from the person's life. This is beneficial in a different way because it relieves a person from the reminder of the emotional pain they endured due to the breakup.

The book discussed the idea of temporary inflation in the example of game tickets and other events. The engagement ring example is the exact opposite. The price is significantly reduced from the original retail selling price. With a higher incentive for the seller to get rid of it in a timely manner, the price is temporarily deflated. In other words, the seller wants to get rid of the ring so much that the ring is devaluated, though only for the present time.

There is a third situation that involves something other than financial and emotional incentives to sell a good. Sometimes there is a need to sell a good in order to allow a person to become better off. Economists are always looking to be better off, so this example is based on such a perspective. If someone finds a need to sell one of their assets in order to be better off, this provides a compelling reason for someone to engage in the resale of a good.

For example, let's consider the resale of a used car. The car that is being sold is ten years old, and the owner has had a lot of problems with it. On average, car repairs cost the owner $1,000 per year, in addition to the fuel, insurance, and routine vehicle maintenance. Because of this, the owner cannot afford to pay for the car anymore. As a result, selling the car becomes a need for the owner because it is too much of a financial burden.

The burden of the car loan plus the unexpected repairs was

simply too much to bear. Thus, by selling the vehicle, the liability is removed. The need to remove the automobile loan from the personal finances of the owner drives the resale of the car. In this instance, it is likely that the car will resale for a price driven by demand for used cars. In other words, car makes and models are a personal choice for the owner. Because preferences different greatly among individuals, the demand for a car is determined by the buyers in the market.

Additionally, the variability of makes and models helps to determine the range of demand. In other words, the quality of a vehicle significantly varies across all of the types of cars in the market.

The number of people who purchase cars within a given range is normally distributed. The variability in the retail prices range from a minimum of a few hundred dollars for a very low-quality used car to a few hundred thousand dollars for a luxury sports car. However, a car is something most people consider to be only one expense as a part of an overall budget. People who are on a limited income need to be conscious of the percentage of their budget that they are devoting to their car purchase.

The distribution of purchases reflects this theory. The vast majority of consumers purchase vehicles in the retail price range of $5,001 to $10,000. A small compact car can be purchased brand new at the upper end of this range. At the lower end, a fairly decent used car can be purchased. Any car in this range is an average "affordable" vehicle on the annual national average salary for a single consumer.

The average American wage earner in a non-family household in 2008 was $29,964. In 2009, the average increased to $30,444. Following this income structure, the average vehicle in this price range accounts for approximately 25 percent of the total household income. Therefore, the car is generally affordable to a buyer who falls in this income bracket.

The person who has the car for resale because they cannot afford to make the payments anymore must consider each of these factors in selling the car. Because the additional money needed for repairs became unaffordable for the owner, there is a timely need to sell the car. Currently, the owner is unable to pay the bills to maintain ownership of the car. This means that even if the demand is low, the strong necessity to sell outweighs the typical pricing structure.

It is extremely difficult to measure the demand for used cars, especially when they are sold directly from owner to buyer. There are few records that help us to determine how many people are shopping for used automobiles. Without a steady flow of buyers in the variable market, the owner of the car has a large incentive to sell the car to the first (and sometimes only) offer they receive. The financial burden would be lifted, and this would remove the need to sell the vehicle.

If the owner chooses not to sell the vehicle to the first person who makes an offer, they run the risk of not receiving another offer; this is similar to the example of selling the condominium earlier in the book. The financial need pressing down on the owner has a large influence on the decision of whether to sell or not. Because the demand is almost immeasurable for a lack of statistics, immediate demand in the form of a quick offer is less price sensitive than a normal demand structure.

The demand structure of any good is determined by the method by which the good is sold. If a good is resold, there are multiple demand foundations that can occur, as shown in the examples. The previously presented goods (houses, cars, etc.) have all been tangible goods, but there is a high demand for intangible goods as well. The majority of the time, intangible goods can only be sold once, since the purchaser can only use them once. One of the largest current trends in intangible goods is the online dating website.

How Can Intangible Goods Bring Consumers Together?

Online dating websites provide a medium by which people can meet others within their geographical area. The websites charge a monthly (or sometimes multi-monthly) subscription fee to virtually "rent" space on the website. Members create an online personal profile that provides information about their likes, dislikes, activities, background, and more in order to find a mate. The interactive forum provides a method for individuals to look at other people's profiles to see if they might be compatible. In this way, the online dating site replaces the typical meetings of dates in bars, restaurants, or through mutual friends.

When online dating first began, there was a negative stigma associated with meeting strangers off of the Internet. Since then, however, things have drastically changed. According to www. grabstats.com, approximately 40,000,000 Internet users engage in at least one online dating site each year. This means that about 40 percent of the U.S. population (presumably the single population) uses one or more online dating sites. The massive increase in the number of users has also attributed to the success of the dating websites because the more users there are, the more subscription fees the sites collect.

The Center for Disease Control reports that there were 2,157,000 people married during 2008. Online introductions accounted for 120,000 of the total marriages in 2008, an estimated 6 percent. In a society full of skeptical consumers, this is a significant increase in successful relationships in a short period of time.

Obviously, millions of Americans are looking for love. Online dating forums create a simplistic medium for people to introduce themselves and interact with a variety of people in a quick, convenient, and rather anonymous way. While this service is a pliable option to replace the local watering hole for all of the cupids in the U.S., it is also a cash cow for the owners and operators of the companies who host the sites.

The online dating industry is worth approximately $1.049 billion annually. Even at this already overwhelmingly huge amount of revenue, the growth rate is still around 10 percent per year. This makes online dating the largest Internet service industry, a monstrosity of a business, even though it delivers no tangible goods to consumers. The only delivery to the consumer is the provision of a forum in which people can meet each other. Still, subscribers are willing to pay significant amounts of money for the chance to find love. For example, Match.com is one of the largest and most popular online dating websites. The website advertises that members can search for free, and this is true. Consumers can sign up, create a profile, and search other members' profiles at no charge or risk. If they want to interact with other member profiles via personal or private messages, they will be asked to pay for this service and make a financial commitment.

Match.com offers "deals" for longer periods of commitment to the website. At the time of this writing, for a one-month subscription, a user is charged approximately forty dollars. If the user is willing to pay for an extended period of six months, there is a discount, as the charge is only about twenty-five dollars per month, regardless of whether or not the user finds a relationship at any point during that timeframe.

Members who sign up on such websites are generally willing to pay according to how much optimism they have when it comes to finding the "perfect" mate online. By joining the website and paying money to do so, the consumer is suggesting that they believe the site will offer them the potential of meeting someone. Although there is no exchange of a tangible good for the payment, the demand for this product is driven by consumer perception. The financial commitment that a consumer makes to the website confirms that the individual believes this type of dating has the potential to lead them to finding someone they would not otherwise be able to encounter via conventional means.

There are 40,000,000 users who willingly pay for these services every year. This colossal number indicates that consumer perception about the good being delivered is highly positive. Unfortunately, there is a delta in the actual good being delivered versus the perceived delivered good. In this case, the perception of the delivered good is a user successfully meeting a significant other and forming a relationship; however, the actual delivered good is merely the rented profile space online to allow a person to market themselves to the vast single community in hopes of pinpointing Mr. or Miss Right.

It is no mere coincidence that consumers follow this thought process when it comes to online dating, but what creates this sense of guaranteed success with online dating websites? Is there a higher probability that someone on the Internet is seeking a relationship more than someone at a bar? Do the people who post profiles online represent a different segment of the population than those who choose to go bar-hopping on the weekends? That answer is undetermined. There are a few key issues to take into consideration in order to answer these questions.

First, advertisements play a large role in a customer's perception of what goods they will actually receive. Most of the large online dating websites advertise via television commercials and social media websites, as well as on billboards, in magazines, and anywhere else where they think they will reach their target audience (40 percent of the entire adult population in the United States). Most of the advertisements include "actual" examples of current or past users of the dating site, serving as their samples of success and proof of the value of their service.

Two major attributes of the samples presented during these advertisements should be noted: physical appearance of the couple and atmosphere and the success stories they present. I will not venture to use the word "all," but the vast majority of the couples in the advertised examples are attractive individuals. The advertised "sampling" suggests to consumers that the physical characteristics of the couple are standard for that website. If a consumer sees physically attractive individuals in the commercial or banner, they will automatically assimilate those people to that website.

Similar to models for any brand, the posed individuals are going to attract the consumer. When it comes to dating, the physical characteristics of individuals are exceptionally important, and they will make a difference when a consumer is choosing which dating site to subscribe to. Although it is not the only factor, the first impression that a user experiences through an online medium is the photograph. Therefore, it is vital for the websites to cater to that in their advertising.

The atmospheres illustrated in many of the commercials on television are centered in upscale restaurants with mood lighting, cloth table settings, and tea-light candles glistening in the background. The commercials show dates between engaging individuals who laugh and enjoy the presence of the person they are sitting across from. This sends a direct message to consumers that this is the dating experience they will receive if they sign up for the website.

The second major attribute of the advertising scheme for online dating is the portrayal of an abundance of success stories. Every couple featured in a dating website advertisement portrays a carefree, happy relationship. Commercials feature couples who depict a brief anecdote of their fairytale relationship, from first date to wedding day. The couples are exorbitantly happy and describe their experiences with ease and glee.

For anyone who has ever been in a relationship (which includes the vast majority of all breathing adults and some teens in the United States), we all know that commitments between two people require hard work, dedication, and selfless sacrifice for the other person. Maybe the dating website advertisers have simply overlooked the need to include these additional distinctions or maybe not; after all, the goal is to sell subscriptions.

The characteristics of advertising to the online dating audience are strategic and intended to divulge primarily positive elements of online dating to consumers. In other words, consumers digest a perceived image of an exceptionally high rate of matchmaking in the Web-based deliverable. The advertisements tell a story about how success comes "naturally" in the online dating forum, but how accurate is this portrayal of success?

Match.com reports that an average of twelve couples get engaged or married every day after initially meeting on their website. This means that on average, 4,380 engagements and marriages each year stem from Match.com. At the same time, Match.com members go out on approximately 6,000,000 dates per year.

If you mesh these statistics together to identify how many of the 6,000,000 dates turn into successful marriages, the number is shocking. These numbers indicate that the success of dating relationships leading to marriage is only 7/100 of 1 percent! Of course this statistic is not mentioned in the advertisements.

Advertising creates a need for consumers, but what else drives the perceived success rates for consumers? A second critical piece of information to consider with the success of online dating websites is the type of consumer who purchases a subscription and actively uses it. Nearly anyone can afford for a one-month subscription, indicating that there is not the factor of financial prohibition. Then again, anyone of the legal age can spend forty dollars to meet someone at a bar, so what is the difference?

The difference between the two mediums of meeting people is the intent of the consumer in both arenas. If someone voluntarily signs up for a dating website, it would be logical to assume that the consumer wants to find a date. This person would not sign up for the website if they did not have any intention of meeting other people on the website who are likewise interested in dating.

Typically, people enter a bar for a different reason. Perhaps they are out with friends or family, just to have fun. There is not necessarily an intention of finding a date when someone enters a bar (or any other social event). While some people do meet their significant others in social situations, there is not a preconceived notion or intent to do so in most cases.

Although there is a difference, the success statistics present a factual representation of what is actually occurring in the dating market. The demand for a date is obviously much greater than the demand for marriage because of the date-to-marriage ratio. Consumers sign up for the websites with the intention of meeting a significant other. Though there is no absolute guarantee that this will happen, the possibility that it may happen is enough for a person to subscribe.

A third characteristic of success to deliberate is the ability to sift through photos and profiles of many people who have similar interests, beliefs, and values. If a person meets someone in a restaurant or bar, the initial chemistry between two people is limited to a purely physical connection. The atmosphere in a bar or restaurant typically tends to be loud and boisterous. This makes it difficult to actually connect with someone intellectually or to get to know them on a deeper level.

Online dating, on the other hand, presents an ability to be matched with other people who are extremely similar to a user. After users input their information into the website to build their personal profiles, their answers are compared against the answers of others. In addition to the profile, some dating websites require people to answer a series of get-to-know-you questions pertaining to their dating rituals and habits in the past. One dating website, www.OkCupid.com, asks exceptionally relevant questions:

- "Do you think it's a necessity for you to communicate every day with the significant other in some mode (be that via e-mail, phone, or in person)?"

- "In your opinion, is contraception ethically wrong?"

- "Regardless of future plans, what is more interesting to you right now, sex or true love?"

- "Have you smoked a cigarette in the last six months?"

- "Could you date someone who is really messy?"

- "Could you date someone who does drugs?"

- "Would you strongly prefer to go out with someone of your own skin color/racial background?"

- "How important is religion/God in your life?"

- "Jealousy: healthy or unhealthy, in the context of a relationship?"

- "Should evolution and creationism be taught side by side in public schools?"

Most people would agree that these questions pertain to intrinsic information that will help build the fundamentals of a solid relationship. There are a plethora of other questions that pertain to religious beliefs, importance of family in a relationship, values, and other more intimate inquiries.

The website takes the answers to these questions and automatically creates a match percentage between two users based on similarities and differences between the two people's answers and the personal information in their profiles. The purpose of this is to closely match people who have a better chance of getting along, based on the answers they provide. Subscribers utilize these tools in order to find more suitable, compatible people to date.

The credibility of this system is only as good as the quality of the answers that users provide. If a user decides to put false information into the questionnaire, they will have less of a chance of finding someone they are very compatible with. On the other hand, if someone is extremely honest and accurate with the information they provide (and so is the person or people they are matched with), this can be an extremely valuable tool to find people that share very similar values.

A final point to consider is that consumers using the websites are actively engaging both their time and financial resources into seeking a potential mate on the website. When someone takes such initiative to find a mate, they are clearly more personally invested in this task than a person who randomly shows up at a bar or restaurant, not necessarily expecting or hoping to meet anyone. Since dating site subscribers pay out of their pockets to be involved with the service, clearly they have some intention of finding someone. Their financial commitment to the site indicates that they are looking for a shared personal commitment with someone else and not just looking to have a drink with someone.

Although it's not always accurate, one can assume this means users care more about finding a significant other than a random person at a social event. The online dater is actively seeking someone to fulfill a role in their life.

A subscriber needs to sign up to the website in order to gain access to the communication portion of the website. Of the online dating websites I looked at, the average person invests $32.13 per month. Compared to a typical bill at a local bar or restaurant for a night out, this is a relatively low cost good for a month of service.

A consumer has a wide variety of websites to choose from according to the list, and this is not even close to being all of the available sites on the Web. Each has specific characteristics, and if a consumer has specific preferences or interests, they can choose the website that attracts other individuals with similar interests to theirs.

For example, www.JDate.com boasts being "the premier Jewish singles community online." Therefore, if someone has a religious affiliation with Judaism, they can potentially find others on the website who hold similar beliefs. Every website has something that makes it unique amongst the hundreds of dating sites on the Web. Are these distinctive, exclusive qualities driving part of the perceived success of the websites?

Though this provides the ability for a subscriber to be extremely selective with the traits and beliefs of the person they are seeking, it is not proven to be the solution to finding the perfect mate online. None of these attributes debated throughout the text above are exclusively successful, but the overall concept and tools integrated into the system facilitate an efficacious medium. It is critical to remember that this is still a business, and it generates revenue through a unique demand structure. An online dating subscription is an intangible good. It cannot be resold, so the demand is always organic in the market.

The profit generated by these companies from the millions of subscribers is driven by an emotional tie to the chance to find love. The website administrators know this and use it to create a demand in the market. This demand is the key to the success of this business. The companies use persuasive advertising, anecdotal success stories, a relatively low-cost product, and a unique offering specific to the user to create a demand for a good that might not even currently exist.

Really, economics is a simple game of supply and demand. The resale of goods influences the supply and demand for the new goods market as well. Depending on what the good is, it has the potential to generate a large amount of revenue. On the contrary, it can also have little to no resale value. Goods are all different, but they all share a similarity of demand. The difference is how and where that demand is generated.

Chapter Seven

How Can Framing Impact a Consumer's Decision-Making Process?

Consumers make hundreds of choices every year on the various products they purchase from grocery stores. Supermarkets play home to a plethora of brands, styles, versions, and types of every different food that one might imagine. Consumer choice of one versus the other is completely dependent on the preferences of the buyer. What influences these preferences for one brand over another? How do consumers make the choices at retail to determine market patterns?

The previous chapter discussed the concept of the origin of demand for a good. Demand must be generated to drive consumers to select a specific item. For the sake of example, let's consider the cookie industry.

Aside from private label brands, Nabisco Chips Ahoy and Oreo were the two top grossing cookie brands in this segment of the market. Each of the companies (maybe with the exception of the private label) invests millions of dollars each year luring consumers to purchase their products. One way to do this is to specifically appeal to the audience that the product is intended to target. In the case of cookies, the largest captive audience for this industry is children.

In order to gain the acceptance (and probably incessant begging) of children for the cookies, companies have to frame the food as a "need" for the children instead of just a "want." The difference between these two designations was explained earlier. One tactic to establish "need" is for companies to convey superheroes and heroines on the packaging to entice children. In other words, the packaging conveys the message that characters with super-strength and courage "need" the cookies in order to perform their audacious feats. This is functional advertising to influence a consumer's choice in goods. Clearly, the cookie industry (especially Nabisco) has mastered this tactic.

Another way to influence a consumer's choice is to use the economic theory of framing. Framing is an interesting concept because there are multiple facets to which it can be applied. The basic premise of the theory is that the way in which an option is presented to a person can and most likely will alter their decision regarding it. In other words, if something is presented with a positive connotation attached, the individual is more likely to choose that rather than the same situation presented with a negative connotation attached, even when the outcome is completely equal.

To further explain this, people make their decisions within the overall context in which they are provided. People are mentally incapable of making unbiased decisions if they have previous knowledge about a situation. If they know a decision is bad for them based on past experiences, they will ultimately choose to avoid that situation again. In order to explicate this theory in laymen's terms, let's use a simplistic example generated from two psychologists who introduced the concept of cognitive bias among people.

In 1981, Amos Tversky and Daniel Kahneman performed a simple framing experiment by asking subjects (similar to how I was tested in the experiment mentioned at the beginning of the book) about their preferences for a situation. They staged the experiment by providing the subject with one situation, followed by two possible outcomes. This was a sequential experiment performed with two different groups of subjects to determine the outcome. The background information given to both groups of participants was as follows:

"Imagine that the U.S. is preparing for the outbreak of an unusual Asian disease, which is expected to kill 600 people. Two alternative programs to combat the disease have been proposed. Assume the exact scientific estimates of the consequences of the programs are as follows."

After this information was provided, the first group of subjects was tested. They were told that there were two programs (Program A and Program B) proposed to combat the disease. The participants were told to choose whichever program they thought would be more beneficial to society. Out of the group of 600 people who were threatened to die from the disease, below were the program outcomes:

Program A: "200 people will be saved."

Program B: "There is a one-third probability that 600 people will be saved, and a two-thirds probability that no people will be saved."

There were outstanding results from the first part of the experiment. The vast majority of subjects (72 percent) favored Program A. The rest of the individuals preferred Program B at only a little over one-quarter of the favored program. Although Program A might appear to have a better outcome because 200 people would be saved, Program B has an expected save of the same number of survivors. One-third of 600 people equates to 200. The difference was simply the wording used to present each option.

The second round of this experiment was with the second group of people. They were given the same background information and told to choose between two different programs (Program C and Program D). Out of the group of 600 people who were threatened to die from the disease, below were the program aftermaths:

Program C: "400 people will die."

Program D: "There is a one-third probability that nobody will die, and a two-thirds probability that 600 people will die."

The second part of the experiment almost mirrored the results of the first. The second group resulted in over 78 percent of the subjects preferring Program D. The remaining people in the experiment expressed their preference for Program C at 22 percent. Once again, although Program C results in the death of 400 people, Program D has the same net result. Two-thirds of 600 people reported dying equates to 400 people.

In both scenarios, a number of people will be saved and a number of people will ultimately die. The difference between the scenarios and programs is simply the way they are worded. For reference, Programs A and C are identical, as are Programs B and D. The first group of subjects was to choose between two programs that both included the concept of a number of individuals being saved. The major implication in Program A was that there was a guarantee that 200 people would be saved.

The key word in this sentence is saved. Saving lives usually has a very positive connotation associated with it. Even though it is apparent that both programs yield the same number of lives saved, the language used embraces different meanings. In Program B, the term probability suggests to subjects that there is still a chance of more than one-third of people dying. Therefore, Program A receives a higher acceptance percentage.

With the second set of subjects, the language is reversed and refers to the number of deaths from the situation instead. Because death is typically associated with negativity, consumers preferred Program D in the second experiment because it refers to a number of people who will not die. Program C, on the other hand, contains the most negative connotation of each of the four programs because it depicts 400 people dying. Although there are still 200 people saved in this instance, this fact is not mentioned, which makes it harder for people to conceptualize it.

In this simplistic model, Tversky and Kahneman realistically demonstrated the framing effect. Consumers utilize past experiences to build positive and negative associations with specific words, and this experiment proves the concept to be true.

An additional classic example of framing was studied by

McNeil, Pauker, Sox, and Tversky in 1982. A group of doctors, students, and current patients were given two solutions to consider for the treatment of lung cancer: surgery or radiation. The study was framed appropriately to determine how each person would react. This was very similar to the first example presented with the Asian disease.

The group of participants was split into two distinct cohorts. Cohort A surveyed the survival percentages for each of the types of treatments for cancer. They were asked to consider that they had cancer and report on which treatment they would prefer for their own health. The data was positioned and delivered to them as noted below:

• Surgical Option: Assume that 100 people have surgery to cure the cancer
  - 90 people live through the operation
  - 68 people are alive after one year
  - 34 people are still living 5 years later

• Radiation Therapy Option: Assume that 100 people use radiation therapy to cure the cancer
  - 100 people live through the radiation treatment
  - 77 people are living after one year
  - 22 people are still living 5 years later.

The framing of this data centers on how many people were alive and living after both treatments. The results for this survey was that 82 percent of people chose the surgical option to cure the cancer, and only 18 percent of people chose radiation therapy for their treatment. Each of the results was framed in the context of the number of people that were living.

Since being alive has a positive essence in society, this frame is positive. The surgical option retained 34 percent of people still living five years later with only 22 percent of the radiation treatment patients living to reach that time period. Because of this, more patients chose to risk a higher percentage to live in the long run rather than in the short run.

Cohort B was the second half of participants who made a decision in the experiment. This group of people received messages that were framed very differently. Instead of concentrating the information on how many people lived through the two treatments, they receive the information in the opposite context. Although the actual numerical data equated to the same, the second cohort examined mortality data of each of the two treatments. The data was positioned and delivered to them as noted below:

- Surgical Option: Assume that 100 people have surgery to cure the cancer
  - 10 people die through the operation
  - 32 people die after one year
  - 66 people die after 5 years later

- Radiation Therapy Option: Assume that 100 people use radiation therapy to cure the cancer
  - 0 people die through the radiation treatment
  - 23 people die after one year
  - 78 people die after 5 years later

The framing of the treatments above centered on death, which holds a negative association in society. As a result, the resulting choices of the subjects for preferred treatment changed. In the negatively framed example above, 44 percent of the people surveyed chose radiation therapy as the treatment plan for curing cancer. The reason for this is that there is an immediate prospect of death for the surgical option. The subjects read this and comprehend it to mean that ten people are destined to die quickly. If they choose radiation therapy, no one will die throughout the actual treatment process.

The reaction garnered from this experiment was based on the background that the participants already had. Cancer is a serious disease, and analyzing the treatment of it is a difficult process. When the outcomes are focused on the positive outlook of living, people will sway their choices one way. By framing the treatment plans negatively with the word "die," consumers will alter what they perceive to be the best possible outcome.

Another important resource besides the health of a person is their purchasing power when it comes to goods they need or want. Unlike the ancient tactics of bartering bearskins for berries, money is the physical representation of buying power and wealth in today's society. As we've learned, economists always assume that more of anything is better. Therefore, the more money a consumer has to spend, the better off they are. In a logical sense, this only means consumers have a larger ability to purchase goods in the market.

Deal or No Deal? How the Framing Effect Changes the Outcome of the Show

Although there are thousands of ways to earn money, an increasingly popular method is to win money on game shows. For instance, the show Deal or No Deal became extremely popular during its run in the U.S., and shortened versions are still running today. The show began in 2005 on NBC Primetime television and immediately gained a large following of viewers and participants.

The premise of the show is that a single contestant starts out with twenty-six cases to choose from. Each case has a different designation of money ranging from $0.01 to $1,000,000 (the value designations are in increments leading up to $1,000,000). The contestant is told to choose one case as "their case," and that case is removed from the other twenty-five, with its designated amount undisclosed; the contestant is not allowed to look at the value that is contained within their chosen case. Next, the contestant plays each round of the game exclusively.

In the first round, the contestant is instructed to choose six cases to open. Once the contestant does that, the values that are contained within those cases are removed from play. Based on the numerical winnings in the leftover cases, the "banker" presents an offer to the contestant, and the player can opt to make a "deal" or "no deal."

From the banker's perspective, the goal is to entice the contestant to take far less than the values left on the game board. At this point in the game, there are still nineteen cases left to open. Therefore, unless the contestant removed all of the largest values from the game, the likelihood of them winning a large amount of money is still relatively high. At this point, the banker wants the contestant to continue the game.

From the contestant's perspective, the goal is to eliminate the majority of the small values on the game board. The cases are chosen at random, and the participant only has the ability to guess cases. If the contestant picks lower-valued cases, this helps to drive the banker's offer up because that means there is a higher likelihood that a higher amount is reserved for them inside the case they have chosen to hold. As long as some high values are still on the table, it behooves the contestant to continue the game.

In each of the consecutive rounds, the contestant has to open fewer cases each time. The banker makes the additional offer based on the numbers left. As more of the high values are revealed, the banker's offers become lower, and vice versa. If the contestant chooses to take the banker's offer and make a "deal," the game ends.

The contestant can also choose "no deal," at which point they will continue selecting cases and eliminating amounts from the board, hoping that theirs contains a large amount. The game continues through all of the cases to determine if the contestant made a financially "good" decision. Unfortunately, many of the contestants on the show end up with far less winnings than they actually could have mathematically earned because they rely too much on keeping the case they initially chose instead of taking the banker's offer or switching it out for the last remaining case at the end.

But why are contestants so attached to that attaché? Simply

put, contestants become emotionally involved and invested in the case that they chose. This is similar to the endowment effect discussed earlier in the book. Contestants retain ownership over the case because they chose it. Since it is something they picked (though blindly), the contestant tends to hold on to it at all costs, sometimes even seemingly bidding against themselves for the sake of keeping that case. Since the cases are numbered one through twenty-six, any contestants select their case based on emotionally significant numbers from their past or numbers that hold some meaning for them, such as birthdates, anniversaries, holidays, ages, etc. The emotional ties make it difficult to believe that other cases might hold higher values.

Statistically, there is a very mathematically rational theory and equation to explain the likelihood of the large values. The following equation summarizes the probability of choosing each of the twenty-six values; this is known as expected value.

$$e(x) = \left(.01 * \frac{1}{26}x\right) + \left(1 * \frac{1}{26}x\right) + \left(5 * \frac{1}{26}x\right) + \left(10 * \frac{1}{26}x\right) + \left(n * \frac{1}{26}x\right) \ldots$$

(x is each of the remaining values of all twenty-six cases)

This equation takes each of the values in the cases and multiples them by the equally likely chance of choosing that value (one case out of twenty-six total cases). Each of the values is then added together for the average expected value that the contestant could receive. Typically, contestants do not apply logical theory to determine how to make their guesses.

Deal or No Deal is an explicit example of the economic framing effect. The contestant starts the game with zero dollars. When a contestant is presented with the offer from the banker after the first round of the game, the person has an important choice to make, and the contestant is faced with a decision between those two choices at each juncture of the game. The producers of the game show use framing to influence the drama and excitement during the show. Let's look at how this is done and explore how both positive and negative framing impacts the decision-making process.

After the first round, assuming that the $1,000,000 case is still in play, there are nineteen cases left on the floor. Let's assume that the banker offers the contestant a sum that is designated by x. The choices are framed as "Would you rather..."

Would you rather?
"...have a 73.1% (19 cases left divided by 26 cases total) of winning $1,000,000?"   OR   "...be guaranteed x dollars that the banker is offering?"

Because this is centered on the concept of "winning," the framing has a positive connotation. This presents a challenge to the contestant because they are invested in the 73.1 percent chance of winning $1,000,000, though this is not actually what the probability of winning that amount of money equates to. Instead, this percentage is the probability that the contestant will actually win the value of one of the nineteen cases left, whatever that value may be. It is framed as the $1,000,000 percentage because we assume the $1,000,000 case is still left in play and could be the contestant's chosen case. Realistically, the probability of winning the million is now 1/19 cases, or a 5.3 percent chance of winning $1,000,000, which is significantly less. The framing of this can help to sway a contestant to keep playing the game so that the payout ends up being far less than it would have been.

Depending on how much drama the show producers want to convey to the audience, the framing effect can be used in a negative context as well. For instance, wording can be used to convince a contestant that the best choice is to take the banker's offer. Consider the same situation as presented above, only delivered in a negatively framed message. Let's assume that the contestant is presented with the same offer from the banker of x dollars. The choices are framed as "Would you rather..."

Would you rather?
"…have a 26.9% chance of losing everything?"
OR
"…forego x dollars that the bank is currently offering at the end of the round?"

In this case, the negatively framed choices are both phrases that indicate the contestant giving up all of the money. Because the contestant wants to win money, this could literally scare them into taking the deal. The show host, who acts as a go-between for the banker and the contestant, might pose a very leading question such as, "Is it really worth the risk to forego x dollars that the banker is willing to offer?" In addition, the host can suggest that specific offers are really good and that he would accept if it were his decision. Framed in a negative context, his personal opinion could influence the contestant one way or another.

The show does not reveal that the chances of winning the game are purely based on probability. With the knowledge of the expected value, the likelihood is somewhat easier to determine. If someone is going to be a contestant, they should consider how questions are framed to them on the show. The rules of the game also ensure that luck plays an integral role, for there is no way to actually know what amounts are hidden inside the cases.

Framing is strategic in influencing a person's decision-making process one way or the other. It occurs constantly in society, game shows and consumer goods markets to name just a couple examples. As we learned from the cookie example at the beginning of the chapter, there are many consumer goods in the supermarkets that are positively framed to consumers to entice a purchase. As the kids are running up and down the cookie aisle begging for their favorite sweets, parents are generally more focused on purchasing healthier items that fall into the more basic food groups. Protein sources, such as some forms of beef, are precise samples of the framing effect.

Purchasing ground beef is a relatively quick process in a

supermarket. In many grocery stores, there is a refrigerated section of prepackaged ground beef, labeled and priced according to the meat grade. Accompanying the price sticker on the package is usually a label indicating the percentage of fat in the specific cut of beef to help consumers decide on their purchases.

According to the United States Department of Agriculture (USDA), there are strict regulations regarding the percentage of fat included in a ground meat package. The USDA website summarizes the requirements for the packages as follows:

"The contractors will establish a target average of 15 percent fat for all ground beef products except for the ground beef patties NTE [Not To Exceed] 10 percent fat and ground lean beef patties. The upper and lower specifications limits will be 18 and 12 percent fat respectively. The target fat content will be declared on the shipping container label and the nutrition facts panel."

Although the government requires this information, it is also used to frame the meat that the consumer is purchasing. The requirement from the USDA is that the information is present on the packaging, clearly visible to the consumer. Retail outlets utilize this to their advantage to influence shoppers to purchase one product or another. Let's see how.

Meat is an expensive commodity. The beef-to-fat ratio drives the price that retail stores will charge. A higher percentage of fat in any given package yields a cheaper cost. The fat is used as filler to magnify the amount of product a consumer is receiving. Therefore, stores will frame the non-fat part of the meat in a healthier context to encourage consumption of the good while being able to offer competitive pricing.

Most grocery stores package ground beef to be sold in their outlet. Because this is regulated by law, stores are obligated to report the amount of fat contained in the package on the front panel. Many people strive to eat healthy to prolong their own lives and the lives of their families. As the growth of overweight people in the United States rises, this becomes an even more glaring restraint. The amount of fat influences people's purchases because of their personal health concerns.

There is a strong national movement toward a healthier lifestyle. Reports from the Center for Disease Control pin-point the extremely high rate of obesity infiltrated throughout the United States.

Obesity is associated with gaining too much weight in the form of fat. Since language (or wordage) is the key to the framing effect, this is a critical piece to this puzzle. Society puts a negative connotation with the word "fat" because it infers that someone will reach obesity. On the contrary, most antonyms of the word fat (i.e. skinny, lean, thin, slim, or slender) are positively associated with being healthy. In terms of economic framing, retailers must consider how they frame the contents on the packaging.

For example, let's assume that a consumer is in the market to purchase a package of ground beef. The consumer walks through the refrigerated section of the store to the beef and starts looking at the packaging. The summary of what the consumer is looking at is the following:

- Brand A contains a statement on the front of the package that states "80% lean meat."

- Brand B contains a statement on the front of the package that states "20% fat."

Although these two brands contain the exact same amount of fat per package, the health conscious consumer is going to associate Brand A to be healthier. The focus for this packaging is on the lean portion of the meat. Since the word "lean" is a synonym for thin, consumers will connect these two words together in their mind. The wording on Brand B is focused on the amount of fat in the product. The ratio is still largely lean meat, but the percentage of fat represented will induce the concept of being unhealthy.

This situation is extraordinarily similar to the Asian disease example presented in the book. When individuals are biased to both positive and negative connotations from their past experiences, they cannot help but apply these to the future. In the case of beef, the words described on the packaging can alter a person's opinion on a product.

An additional consumer product that is extremely popular among young people is an Italian classic. Pizzerias all over the United States produce millions of pies each year that are consumed. The industry is worth approximately 30 billion dollars per year with an estimate of 69,000 restaurants nationally. The market for this product is highly desirable.

Ordinarily pizzerias have two options for people that order a pizza as a take-out order. Consumers can either pick the pizza up from the store by ordering it ahead of time on the phone as a "carry-out" order. This is a relatively inexpensive way to distribute a pizza because once it is made, the consumer actually spends the time and money to come and pick it up. They pay for their order and leave the restaurant.

The other option is to have a delivery person bring the pizza to the residence in which it was ordered from. This requires the pizzeria to hire an additional employee to deliver the pizza to the consumer. It also requires the driver to pay extra money for gas, and they are unable to perform more work at the restaurant when they are driving to different deliveries. The additional effort, money, and time spent in the delivery process incentivize restaurant owners to offer deals to encourage customers to carry out their order. On average, carry-out orders are relatively less expensive than a delivery order.

Because of this, pizzerias will offer special deals to customers pertaining to the distribution method of the pizza. The restaurant will frame it to create a positive association with a carry-out order. For example, a restaurant will advertise that a consumer will save 10% off of their order if they decide to pick it up from the restaurant. This reduction is the price can be a significant saving for consumers. Saving money has a positive connotation because that additional money can be spent on another need (or want) of the consumer.

As previously mentioned, economists assume that more is always better, and this savings is ultimately considered to be better. This takes the same amount of money that a consumer has and expands what they are able to purchase with it similar to the extreme coupon methods mentioned earlier in the book.

On the other hand, the restaurant will also charge a 10% additional fee for a pizza to be delivered in order to cover the costs. Additional fees have a negative connotation because the consumer is paying 10% more for the pizza than the pizza is actually worth (or the regular price of the pie). By paying more for the delivery service, the consumer forgoes other needs (or wants) that they could be spending this additional money on.

Depending on how the restaurant decides to frame the service, consumers will react to it differently. The ability of a consumer to have their food delivered at their doorstep might outweigh the financial costs of having that done. It is completely dependent upon consumer preference.

By framing the good this way, the restaurant owner is framing the distribution method to benefit the profit of the restaurant. As an incentive, the owner is providing a reduced price pizza just for the time and effort of picking the pizza up. Although this seems basic, pizzerias offer these types of deals regularly.

In addition, it is vital for pizza restaurant owners to remain aware of any promotions that their competition is running. For pizzerias within a fairly tight geography, price can mildly dictate where consumers purchase their pies from. If one pizzeria offers a discounted deal for carry-out orders of 10%, other pizzerias within the market are pressured to do the same to remain competitive. When competing restaurants do not offer some sort of deal or discount on their products, they lose incremental business from random price driven consumers. The more pizzas sold, the higher the volume profit will be.

Another extremely popular, readily available good discussed in various segments throughout the book is cigarettes. Cigarettes are another product that can adhere to the framing effect. Consumers spend millions of dollars on this addictive product every year. In 2010, the average retail price of a pack of cigarettes in the United States was approximately $4.80 which includes federal, state, and municipal excise taxes.

The CDC reported in 2009 that 20.6% of all adults (which equates to 46.6 million people) smoke cigarettes. The average amount of money spent per year (assuming that on average people are smoking one pack of cigarettes per day) is approximately $223,680,000. If the high prices aren't enough to gouge consumers and negatively influence their decision process, the government is planning to use framing to deter people from using the product.

The United States Food and Drug Administration (FDA) announced that beginning in September 2012, every cigarette pack, carton, and all advertisements were required to contain "larger, more prominent cigarette health warnings." The goal of this action is to help prevent more youth from starting smoking and encourage current smokers to quit. The FDA website (www.FDA.gov) provides examples of what a new pack of cigarettes will be required to look like when this law is implemented.

Because tobacco is a legal good for adults (those who are eighteen and older), it is available in over 200,000 retail outlets throughout the country. The consumption of cigarettes is a choice that an adult has the right to make. By implementing these changes to the packaging, the government is creating awareness that the product is a negative life decision for one's health. The warning "smoking can kill you" sends consumers a clear message of negative health risks associated with the decision to consume the product.

This is a prime example of framing in a very concise message on the packaging. The word "kill" here is rooted with negative connotation in society, as it is clearly associated with death. Obviously, the message signifies that cigarettes are "bad," and the goal of the packaging is to discourage people from using the product. By negatively associating the good with death by placing the word "kill" directly on the package, the framing effect says that consumers will be more apt to deny themselves the cigarette.

The packaging purposely does not include any good or

positive associations or even less harsh ones. If these were included, consumers would be more accepting of the product, albeit avid smokers will still purchase and use the product in spite of the warning signs plastered all over the advertisements and packaging. The framing effect here is completely direct to send a consumer only one message: "If you buy and use this product, it will kill you."

In the course of my research on these packaging changes, I came across a second form of the framing effect associated with this particular product. A similar message (that smoking will kill you) is mimicked on the Center for Disease Control website through the language used to describe the statistics relating to cigarette use. The website posts statistical information regarding some of the illnesses related to smoking cigarettes. The information below is taken verbatim from the CDC website, copied exactly so as to demonstrate the language used in framing:

- "Worldwide, tobacco use causes more than five million deaths per year, and current trends show that tobacco use will cause more than eight million deaths annually by 2030."

- "In the United States, tobacco use is responsible for about one in five deaths annually (i.e., about 443,000 deaths per year, and an estimated 49,000 of these tobacco-related deaths are the result of secondhand smoke exposure)."

- "On average, smokers die thirteen to fourteen years earlier than nonsmokers."

There are two distinctly negative words used repeatedly to report these grim statistics: "death" and "die." People are biased to these words because death is naturally something humans try to avoid, if at all possible. These statistical reports are framed precisely around the words to convey the harmful nature of the product. The language used helps to tell the story of how dangerous cigarettes are for human consumption.

For a comparison, the factual data could be reported from a positive outlook by conveying the number of smokers who actually live long, healthy lives while using the product. The language would vary to promote phrases such as "the health of a smoker" and "the life of a smoker." Though this would still allow reporting of the same statistical data, the framing of positively associated words such as "health" and "life" would convey a different, more positively associated tone to a reader.

The overarching goal of the change is to reduce the number of smokers in the United States. The image shows someone who died from using the product. The government imposition of this new law changes how people perceive the side effects of the product. If people retain a negative response to them, they are less likely to consume the product.

"Click It or Ticket": The Most Successful Seatbelt Enforcement Campaign of All Time

Just as consumers are less likely to purchase cigarettes that are framed with a photo of a dead person, positive reinforcements through framing can help to shape other habits and behaviors. One highly controversial risk that many Americans take every day is riding in motor vehicles without wearing their seatbelt. In most states, it is illegal to drive or ride in a moving vehicle without a properly fastened safety belt, yet thousands of people refuse to wear them. Thus, drivers and passengers risk being injured or even killed in an automobile accident.

The CDC reports that seatbelts are known to decrease serious automobile crash-related injuries and deaths by about 50 percent. There is not really any way to prevent an accident from happening (thus, why it is called an "accident"), but the risk of injury or death from a collision is greatly reduced when a seatbelt is worn. This concept appears to be relatively simple and convenient. It takes minimal effort for a person to strap a belt across their body before putting a car into drive. Surprisingly, the percentages of people who actually use seatbelts are fewer than expected, considering that such a massive increase in safety can be had (50 percent less chance of being injured or dying is a pretty impactful number) just by performing a simple gesture prior to driving or riding in a car.

The total number of people reported in 2007 to regularly wear their seatbelts was 82 percent, up by one point in 2008. Considering their ease of use and the fact that seatbelts are readily available in every vehicle because they are required by law, why isn't this number closer to 100 percent? Did the 17 percent of people in 2008 who chose not to wear their safety belts think themselves invincible or that they were not susceptible to the risk of a car wreck? It is difficult to pinpoint a single answer to these questions.

In 1978, a study was done regarding seatbelt use and how people perceive the value of safety belts. Paul Slovic, Baruch Fischoff, and Sarah Lichtenstein performed specific experiments to examine seatbelt use. When the experiments were performed, only about 15 percent of the population used seatbelts. The report from Slovic, Fischoff, and Lichtenstein indicated that the small percentage of use was due to the miniscule probabilities that a driver would actually be involved in an accident.

When consumers thought they were too invincible for an accident to happen to them, they were unwilling to put the additional effort in to wearing a seatbelt. The researchers decided to perform a framing experiment with two groups of subjects. The first set of participants was provided with statistics regarding the probability of the occurrence of an accident on a per-trip basis. In other words, they were informed of the statistical likelihood that someone might get in a car accident on a single trip.

The experiment reported that a fatal accident only occurs in 1 out of 3,500,000 trips that a person takes. This means the probability that someone would be killed in a car accident on a per-trip basis is almost obsolete. The report also noted that on a per-trip basis, there is only a 1 in 100,000 trip probability that a person would incur injury from an accident. These statistics did not compel people to wear their seatbelts, and these statistics drove the results from the first group of participants in the experiments.

The scientists knew these numbers did not pose an accurate picture of the dangers associated with not wearing a seatbelt. In order to provide a bigger picture, they took the average number of trips per year (which equated to 40,000) to look at the probability of a car accident in driver's lifetime, and these statistics were presented to the second group of participants in the experiment. The values were much more compelling, as both probabilities greatly increased. The second group of participants was presented with the following statistics. The probability of being killed over the entire driver's lifetime of trips is 1 percent, and the probability of sustaining at least one injury during the same period of time is 33 percent. These massively increased percentages greatly altered the results of the experiment from the group who received these statistics.

After the data set was presented, each group of people was asked to endorse seatbelt laws pertaining to the respective statistics they had received. Less than 10 percent of the first group of participants was willing to actively endorse the laws. On the contrary, in the second group of participants, 39 percent were willing to sanction the laws. The massive jump was due to the framing effect.

Although the information was exactly the same in both cases, it was presented very differently. By pinpointing a smaller data set (the 40,000 lifetime trips of an average driver), the perceived probability of being injured or dying in a car accident drastically increased. From this perspective, consumers were more conscious of the dangers associated with not wearing a seatbelt. The new numbers indicated that there was a one in three chance that someone would be involved in a wreck and incur injury. The large increase from the second set of data was enough to encourage people to change their habits and behaviors.

This change was reflected in the actual increase of seatbelt wearers from 1981 (the time of the experiment) to the present. The CDC reports that the usage rate started at 11 percent in 1981 and was approximately 85 percent by 2010. The number of lives saved from these statistical findings is astonishing.

The framing of this information drastically changed the way the participants viewed the importance of wearing their safety belts. By using statistics to dictate how a seatbelt would influence a person's health and safety, their frequency of use grew exponentially, and many lives were saved.

The framing effect is used in a variety of contexts to convey a message to consumers about a situation. Depending on the goal of the party using the framing effect, the framing can be either positive or negative. Framing can be as simple as changing one word, or it can also encompass a complex statement or phrase. Regardless, the effect that it has on an individual depends completely on their past experiences. This dictates how biases affect an individual's reaction to the framed context. This is an economic tool to enable one party to influence another. The variety of examples displayed how ordinary products are framed to influence consumer behavior.

Chapter Eight

Why Does Comparing Three Goods Change Perspective?

Thus far, we have discussed many things, including the fact that consumers purchase millions of goods each day in the market. Every good is bought to serve different purposes for consumers. Depending on the type of goods a person is buying, the shopper may go through a process to determine which brand or variety is the best one to fit their specific needs. This process can be overly simple or fairly complicated, based on the function of the good being purchased.

For example, a loaf of bread is a key staple for a large number of people. When a consumer is at a grocery store, they have a variety of options when it comes to selecting a loaf of bread. Because this is a relatively inexpensive good and it will diminish as the consumer and their family eats it, a consumer is able to pick up the flavor variety (white, wheat, whole grain, rye, or others) and the brand of their choice quickly and move on to the additional items on their shopping list. If the consumer ultimately changes their mind and decides they want a different kind of brand of bread, they have the ability to do so on their next grocery shopping trip. The purchase choice only lasts a short period of time for this type of good.

Other types of goods are more permanent than food (or other quickly consumable products) because they have a longer life for the consumer. Usually, these goods tend to be more expensive because the purchase is an investment in a good that will be used more than once over a period of time. For example, a flat-screen television is a purchase that is intended to be used for at least a number of years. Flat-screen televisions offer a variety of specifications, looks, sizes, and features, and this helps to create unique characteristics for each brand and model. In order to determine the brand, size, and model of the television most suitable for a person's needs, consumers use a comparison method based on the specifications and price of the television sets they are considering. Customers may be price or quality driven, depending on what is more important to them at the time when they are buying the TV.

If a consumer is driven by quality, this means he or she will be willing to spend a little extra money to get a better product. If they are price driven, consumers are willing to give up quality to cut the cost down a bit. Consumers will narrow their choices within a given price range to two final choices and decide between those two. In fact, quality versus price are the two largest attributes that will influence a consumer's decision between two similar goods. As the quality of a product increases, the price tends to simultaneously increase as well; likewise, as the quality of the product diminishes, there is a notable decline in price in most cases. All products vary, and it is not always simple to make a definitive choice between two televisions. More specifically, if there is not a significant gap between the prices of the two products, the decision can be especially difficult.

The Impact of a Third Wheel: The Asymmetric Dominance Effect

Economists use a decision-making tool called the "asymmetric dominance effect" (also known as the "decoy effect") to help drive a consumer's decision-making process. The premise of the theory is that if two goods are being compared with one another on the basis of price and quality, the additional comparison of a third strategically chosen good will help to determine the best possible outcome for a consumer.

In order to explain this further, let's use a simplistic economic model and apply it to our flat-screen television example. The graph below depicts a generic product comparison between two goods, which we will refer to as X and Y. For this explanation, please assume that the consumer has already narrowed down their two overall choices to Goods X and Y, but the consumer is unsure which good will be a better deal for their needs.

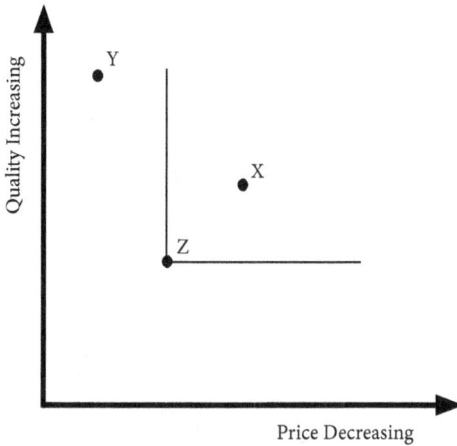

Goods X and Y have mutually exclusive traits, all of which pose an advantage for the end user. Good Y is ranked higher in overall quality, as compared to Good X. The benefit for purchasing Good X, however, is that it is priced quite a bit lower than Good Y.

The asymmetrical dominance effect introduces a third item, Good Z, as an alternative to the original choices. Good Z represents an asymmetric dominance because it is completely dominated by at least one product choice (Good X), but it is not dominated by the other choice in the set (Good Y). Good Z has a much preferred price point as compared to Good Y, but the quality of the product is not equal. When a consumer compares the differences between Goods X and Z, it is apparent that Good X is superior to Good Z in both price and quality. By introducing Good Z into the mix, the comparison between Goods X and Y becomes much simpler for the consumer. Good X is dominant over Good Z, while Good Y is not. In other words, Good Z becomes the driver for a consumer to choose Good X over Good Y. By adding Good Z to the set, consumers have a more apparent awareness of what a great "deal" Good X actually is.

The theoretical explanation can be somewhat confusing, so let's revert back to our original example and assume that a consumer is going to purchase a flat-screen television. The information below is a summary of the specifications for Televisions X and Y:

Television X
• Well-known, trusted global name brand • 55-inch screen / 1080p / 120 Hz / LCD HDTV • Not a smart television • Priced at $799.99 • Received four out of five stars in online customer reviews

Television Y

• Well-known, trusted global brand name
• 55-inch screen / LED / 1080p / 120 Hz / 3D / HDTV
• Smart television features include:
  - Streaming movies from Netflix (subscription required) and CinemaNow
  - Streaming music from Pandora and SiriusXM
  - Watching videos from YouTube
  - Accessing Facebook and Twitter
  - Studying fantasy sports info
  - Reading news, weather, and sports
• Priced at $1,699.99
• Received 4.6 out of 5 stars in online customer reviews

To maintain consistency, the television titles correspond to the original graph above (Good X represents Television X, and so on). Television Y is far superior to Television X in product quality. The product features smart television capabilities, an additional dynamic feature that allows the consumer to access the Internet through the television. Another feature is 3D functionality, and the product has a high customer review rating. However, this television is priced $900 higher than Television X.

There is a huge gap in the quality of the two products because of all of the added features for the product. If a consumer is only comparing these two televisions, it is difficult to determine if the additional $900 is worth the value of the added features. Are the added features worth the additional $900 for the television? Will the specific consumer end up using these luxuries, or do they run the risk of paying a higher price to have them but never really using them once they have the set hooked up at home?

In order to help quantify the features into a dollar amount, the asymmetric dominance effect could be applied to compare one more television.

Television Z
• Generic name brand • 55-inch screen / 1080p / 120 Hz / LCD HDTV • Not a smart television • Priced at $849.99 • Received 4.2 out of 5 stars in online customer reviews

Compared to Television Y, this television offers a superior price, but the quality is not as good. This television does not have any smart television capabilities, nor is it a well-known or recognizable brand. Compared to Television X, this television is inferior in both quality and price because it is generically branded and priced at $150 more than Television X.

This third product comparison proves that Television X is the best choice. It is superior to Television Z in both qualities and superior to Television Y in price. With the addition of Television Z, the value of X becomes much more apparent. By using such an analysis, the consumer relieves themselves of having to make a very difficult decision, as it is rather clear what the right choice is.

Another extremely popular item to consider under the asymmetrical dominance effect is the memory card used in a consumer's digital camera. It is critical that the memory card has enough storage capacity to take all the photographs and video that the consumer wishes to take with their camera. Although the pictures can be downloaded off of the card frequently, it is not always convenient to download pictures just to be able to take additional photos.

There is a wide variety of storage capacity available on these cards, and the corresponding prices increase commensurate with the number of available gigabytes. For this example, let's assume that an average user decides to purchase a digital camera and must buy a memory card for it. In consideration of this, they look at two different sizes. The first consideration set is as follows:

	A	B
Price	$25	$15
Storage	16GB	8GB

Option A offers superior storage capacity because it holds twice the number of gigabytes that Option B does. On the contrary, Option B is superior in price because it is ten dollars less than the larger size chip. For a consumer who is unable to forecast how many pictures or videos they will be taking during a given session, this can be a challenging decision. Should they spend less money but run the risk of missing out on candid pictures? What advantages are there to spending almost double for a larger capacity of photo space?

Consider this same example with the asymmetric dominance effect applied. In this case, we add an Option C:

	A	B	C
Price	$25	$15	$20
Storage	16GB	8GB	4GB

For a consumer, Option B is most definitely the dominant strategy in this mix. The new addition of Option C is superior to Option A on price but significantly inferior on the storage capacity since it holds only one-fourth of the photos that Option A is able to hold. Option C is inferior to option B in both price and storage capacity. This helps the consumer to see that there are no better options than Option B. Option C is inserted into this example to convey the value that a consumer receives with Option B.

This example is highly likely to occur in retail stores. Many stores carry a variety of brands that fall into different pricing brackets. In the case of a digital camera storage chip, the brand is somewhat irrelevant. The chip is put into the camera, and most people do not see it. As long as the chip functions properly, there is no reason to even consider the name brand. Because of this, digital camera chip manufacturers must remain price conscious and competitive with the other brands on the market.

Theoretically, the asymmetrical dominance effect can be applied to many consumer goods. From a consumer's point of view, the theory can be a powerful tool when it comes to putting the value of goods into perspective. Aside from comparing the prices and quality of various goods, it can also be used to help give perspective to consumer preference.

For our next example, let's assume that a couple decides to go out for dinner, and they have a craving for Italian food. Each person has expressed that they are extremely hungry because they both skipped lunch during the day. There is a new Italian eatery that just opened up, purportedly serving the best spaghetti and homemade meatballs in the area. The new restaurant is located forty minutes away from the couple's home.

Because they are extremely hungry, they consider something a bit closer. A fast food Italian chain franchise is located five minutes down the street from them. The food is mediocre at best, but the service is extremely fast. This forces them to make a decision. The following is the matrix to demonstrate the couple's options:

	A	B
Drive Time	40 Minutes	5 Minutes
Quality of Food	Best	Average

Currently, the food at Restaurant A is superior to Restaurant B, but the time it takes to get to the restaurant is inferior to the time it takes to commute to Restaurant B.

When the asymmetric dominance effect is applied to this example, there is an additional option to put consumer preference into perspective. The third restaurant is one the couple visited about a year prior and wants to revisit. They recall that they enjoyed some really great bruschetta as an appetizer, but the restaurant is located in the downtown area of their city. With traffic, it will take a full hour to get there. The following is a matrix integrating the "third wheel" into this decision:

	A	B	C
Drive Time	40 minutes	5 minutes	60 minutes
Quality of Food	Best Spaghetti	Average	Good Appetizers

With the additional time and hassle required to make the commute in heavy traffic, the third option is asymmetrically dominated. Restaurant C requires a longer drive time, rendering it inferior to Restaurant A. It also only serves "good" appetizers, which are inferior to the "best spaghetti" that Restaurant A is known for. Restaurant B is superior to C when considering the time of commuting, but it is inferior in quality of food. When the couple analyzes the additional option of Restaurant C, the forty-minute drive to Restaurant A doesn't seem so bad for such great food.

Consumer preference can also be measured in other contexts besides goods. Consider the United States presidential election of 1988, for example. The two main candidates for the Republican and Democratic parties were George W. Bush and Michael Dukakis, respectively. Although this election resulted in a Republican landslide win with a 426 Republican to a 111 Democrat electoral vote, consumer preference played a large role in the initial candidate nomination.

The Democratic nomination was based on the outcome of the 1984 candidate profile, and Walter Mondale had been nominated as the presidential candidate in the prior election. He supported policies such as the New Deal and based his political decisions on a liberal viewpoint. When he was defeated for the seat of the presidency, the Democratic Party wanted to change their stance for the future. In essence, the Democrats were on the lookout for some new blood, someone fresh who would adhere to more left-wing beliefs. Governor Michael Dukakis was known for extremely liberal ideas such as not making the Pledge of Allegiance a mandatory recitation in American classrooms. On the contrary, the Republican Party was much more conservative in their beliefs. President George W. Bush campaigned for law and order to keep the conventional viewpoints of prior President Ronald Reagan. President Bush was a seasoned candidate with a lot of political experience under his belt.

For United States citizens preparing to vote, the asymmetrical dominance effect applied directly to this presidential campaign. The two basic characteristics for each candidate can be summarized by the matrix below, and each of these was critical for consideration in the candidates:

	Republican	Democrat
Experience	Seasoned Veteran	Fresh
Viewpoint	Conservative	Liberal

When a citizen has to consider who to vote for at the polls, particularly in a presidential election, the decision can be tricky. In order to influence the decision-making process, a third-party candidate from the Libertarian party was introduced. Ron Paul was the representative for this candidacy, and the Libertarian party was split between a conservative wing and a liberal wing, with Paul representing the conservative wing of the party. He campaigned and spoke about free market economic policies and targeted his speeches to younger voters, as he believed they represented the future decision-makers and that they needed to be shaped in the present to prepare for the future.

To follow the asymmetric dominance effect, this introduces the third option into play. The following is the matrix with the Libertarian Party added in.

	Republican	Democratic	Libertarian
Experience	Seasoned Veteran	Fresh	Some Experience
Viewpoint	Conservative	Liberal	Conservative

The addition of the conservatively focused Libertarian Party candidate was to illustrate that the Republican candidate was a better choice for a conservative point of view. The Republican candidate dominated with more political experience, a larger following of people, and a stronger conservative background. President George W. Bush campaigned to follow in the footsteps of the conservative take on policy from the previous president, Ronald Reagan. Thus, Americans were able to envision the sense of security that they had grown accustomed to.

This theory helps consumers to compare the value of one good with others by outlining trade-offs from both sides. Consumers are able to better determine if they are receiving a great (or even fair) market deal on a good by paralleling it with others in the market. As explained, it can also be useful to analyze consumer preferences and what holds a higher value for people. In the above example, it was the length of time to travel to a restaurant versus the quality of the food.

The dual comparison method provides a more thorough depiction of the features and benefits of a variety of options. Instead of a consumer only comparing two options, a third is presented to provide a perspective on how valuable the others are. After all, the only way to designate value for a good or service is to determine the value of other similar goods and services. When goods are put into a different perspective, consumers can make an informed decision about the products they plan to purchase, and this is the foundation of economics.

Conclusion

The world is full of useful tools. Many of these tools are physical utensils that give humans the strength to perform unimaginable feats. For instance, a hammer can enable a single man to build a house, a wrench can help us change a car tire in a dangerous situation, and the Jaws of Life can save a victim who is trapped in a car. These literal aids are helpful, but there are also valuable tools that mentally engage consumers.

Mental tools have the weight of 10,000 wrenches or hammers. They invite individuals to think outside the box and challenge the norm. The application of economic theory to the everyday situations mentioned throughout this book has been demonstrative of this point. Economic theory can provide a foundation not only to enable a man to build a house, but also to enable him to successfully sell it when that becomes necessary.

Thus, the examples presented in this book have hopefully highlighted at least a small glimpse of economic understanding for consumers. At one point or another, almost everyone has purchased a gallon of gas, resold or purchased a used item, worn a seatbelt, idolized a professional athlete, started a diet (and possibly ended one), earned a wage as a paid employee, bought a gallon of milk, considered a variety of airlines for an important flight, or used a coupon to receive a discount on a product. I could go on and on, but the point is that economics is part of real life, of the ordinary activities we do every day. Economics is applicable in almost any situation, and knowingly or not, consumers around the globe use this tool constantly to analyze their decisions, big or small. Economics, in its most simplistic forms, drives the world to make rational decisions based on the best possible outcomes for each individual in their specific situation.

Economics may only be a needle in a haystack when compared to the other educational possibilities in the world, but when that needle is found, the possibilities to analyze and learn from economic theories are endless. The best part is that in reality, economics is as simple as eating a meal at McDonald's, reselling a vehicle, identifying how cigarettes are uniquely advertised in the market, or finding a buyer for an engagement ring if a relationship does not work out. In other words, almost any activity we do is intrinsically intertwined with economic theory in some way, whether we realize it or not.

The title of this book is ec·o·nom·ics. This description is purposefully simplified. When I was trying to think of what to title the book, I thought back to the days of grammar school, when I was learning how to spell. My fellow peers and I learned how to break words down into syllables and sound them out. I would spend hours sitting at my kitchen counter with my parents reading words out to help me to practice for my weekly spelling tests. I wrote the words I misspelled on a piece of paper ten times over to help me memorize their correct spellings. For words I was unsure of, I knew that if I took them one syllable at a time and spelled them out, there was a fairly decent chance I would be able to sound them out and spell them correctly. The pieces added together and eventually compiled a word, a metaphor that is overtly perfect for the examples provided in this book. Similar to sounding out the syllables in those difficult-to-spell words, each example you have read is simplistic in nature and easy to understand. By themselves, the examples are just anecdotes and don't mean much, but together, they function to form a whole concept.

The compiled stories, events, and facts you have read here glue economic theory together; thus, the reason I titled this book ec·o·nom·ics, with the syllables broken apart to represent the simplicity of the book. This book should be judged by its cover! Hopefully, it has helped you to literally break economics down into simple, digestible snippets of information for anyone and everyone to enjoy and learn from.

Do you remember the aura of the football stadium that we envisioned at the beginning of the book? For a fan, watching favorite players charge onto the field is an adrenaline-inducing experience. The grass is freshly cut, and the painted team logos are awe-inspiring. The ticket booths and concession stands are filled with employees who gratefully accept money from excited and hungry fans. In return, the clerks provide the fans with bratwurst, French fries, nachos, and another ice cold beer. The atmosphere of the game is one bursting with excitement, entertainment, and enjoyment. Every piece of the puzzle seems to fit together and function seamlessly, without a hitch, in the same way the syllables of a word conjoin to create a meaning for the word. The working parts of the game are glued together to cohesively bind each part, and now you know that the flawlessness of this planning is a function of ec·o·nom·ics.

Epilogue

At the beginning of this book, I challenged you to question everyday occurrences. Are you convinced yet that there really aren't black and white lines drawn to define the situations you encounter? The greater challenge is to think about each of the examples mentioned the next time you engage in them. Question each example and at least try to apply one of the theories from this book.

Ec·o·nom·ics was defined in the introduction of this book as "the science that deals with the production, distribution, and consumption of goods and services, or the material welfare of humankind." I hope what you have read here has alluded to the fact that it is so much more than that. In its most simplistic form, it encompasses and drives society. Each and every example in this book is proof.

I believe in the gray area, reading between the lines, and questioning what the experts have to say. There are always at least two sides to every story or at least two choices for a given situation. Hopefully, this book has provoked you to ask questions, develop opinions, and argue a new outlook on a variety of topics. Economics is full of theories developed by intelligent and forward-thinking individuals who have dared to question the norm. These individuals didn't just accept what they were told; rather, they chose to experiment and research to prove their own theories.

Be one of these people in society! Instead of taking what is already said as being etched in stone, dare to rewrite the story yourself. I know from this experience that it will behoove you to do so.

Acknowledgements

There are literally hundreds of thousands of people to thank for inspiring me to write this book. I would like to personally thank the professors who sparked my initial interest in economics at Indiana University, the many thinkers whose written works inspire my passion to be an author, the historians who savor the moments in life that shape the future, and the ordinary people who continually dare to question the norm and demand more out of life than the status quo. Without the help of all of these people, this book would have not come to fruition.

I would also like to personally thank my friends for supporting me in each and every one of my endeavors. They help me through each feat and are always willing to help me relieve stress at the local watering hole. I am lucky enough to be surrounded by friends whom I consider to be my family.

My parents have encouraged me unconditionally throughout my life, and I am proud to write this book in their honor. Thank you so very much, Mom and Dad, for always being my biggest fans.

I want to thank my sister Stephanie ("Cookies" to me). Without a role model like her, I would never be the person I am today. I couldn't ask for a better best friend and supporter. Love you, Cooks.

Last, but most certainly not least, I want to thank the love of my life, my boyfriend Joe. Anytime I need a smile, I look to you. Thank you for being in my life and for caring so much about my happiness. I am truly a lucky person to have you.

Index

Notes

1. The scientific definition of economics used in the introduction was taken directly from Dictionary.com. There are a variety of definitions for the term economics depending on the context in which it is used. This definition was chosen because it was the most relevant to the meaning of the book. The URL is http://www.dictionary.reference.com/browse/economics.

2. Freakonomics and SuperFreakonomics are two books written by Steven Levitt and Stephen J. Dubner that were mentioned in the first part of the book. The books are both based on empirical data gathered by the authors accompanying their own hypotheses. They discussed topics such as cheating teachers, the relevancy of baby names, and the motivating factors that drive realtors to sell houses. The URL is http://www.freakonomics.com.

3. The United States Center for Disease Control and Prevention (CDC) was a valid source of many of the statistical data referred to in the book on tobacco, cigarettes, nutrition, and obesity. The CDC website has a large variety of facts available that is based on information gathered throughout the United States. The website is a comprehensive conglomeration of health and disease related information for the public. The URL is http://www.cdc.gov.

4. The United States Bureau of Labor Statistics provided information regarding the labor force, unemployment rates, minimum wage, and educational enrollment. Some of the information provided came from graphs, charts, and other pictorial representations of the numbers mentioned in the book. The URL is http://www.bls.gov.

5. The University of North Carolina reported a study regarding the costs of textbooks for students at the home campus and satellite schools. The administrators were concerned enough to determine how much money students were spending on the required textbooks for their classes. They used the statistical information to find solutions to

reduce the costs for books. The URL is http://www.northcarolina.edu/finance/textbooks/2011_Textbooks_Report.pdf.

6. The business information regarding Groupon came directly from the website. Much of the specific information was directly generated from the "profile" portion of the page where users can create a unique request for specific deals that fit their likes and dislikes. The luxury good information for laser hair removal was taken directly from one of the deals that was offered and purchased. The URL is http://www.groupon.com.

7. The New York Times Online article was a perfect fit to analyze the difference in textbook costs for an American version versus the international version of the same book. It provided the information about the two textbooks that were identified. The cost variances were reported directly in the article. The article was written in 2003, but the cost comparison was the main purpose for choosing the article. The fact that the actual costs of the two books now are probably increased with inflation is irrelevant to the example presented in the book. The URL is http://www.nytimes.com/2003/10/21/us/students-find-100-textbooks-cost-50-purchased-overseas.html.

8. The online dating websites mentioned in this book were from first-hand experience with the interactive user forums. There were many different online dating sites that were analyzed in this process, and the most popular and user-friendly sites were the ones included in this text. They were chosen for specific reasons to argue the points mentioned in the text. The URL's included http://www.match.com, http://www.jdate.com, http://www.okcupid.com, http://www.plentyoffish.com, http://www.eharmony.com.

9. The United States Food and Drug Administration (FDA) had ample information on the website regarding tobacco prevention and packaging statistics. Users can view the images that will be depicted on the packs of cigarettes beginning in September 2012. These images are both disturbing and graphic in nature to send the message to smokers that these products are harmful. The URL is http://www.fda.gov.

10. The "Click It or Ticket" campaign that strived to encourage drivers and passengers in cars to wear seatbelts was run by the National Highway Traffic Safety Administration (NHTSA). The website was used to gather data and information about how many people wear their seatbelts and what the mortality rate was of people who did and did not. The URL is http://www.nhtsa.gov.

11. The Prisoner's Dilemma is an economic theory that is deeply rooted in the core of Game Theory. There are many examples besides

the information presented in this book that include environmental challenges between different sectors of the world and education levels among people of the same age. Although I was not able to include all of these examples in the book, the theory is applicable to almost any event where there are two sides making a decision based on the same outcome structure. More in depth descriptions of Game Theory describe what occurs in different markets with additional factors involved.

12. Inflation is an economic term that is applicable to a variety of goods and services, but the premise of it is how it directly affects the purchasing power of individuals who possess currency of any sort. Throughout the world, inflation rates greatly differ depending on how much currency an individual government is willing to flush into a market (and many other conditions that impact the rate of a country. The United States Bureau of Labor Statistics (BLS) has an interesting tool on their website that helps users grasp just how impactful this factor is on their income, savings, and overall purchasing power. The tool allows users to put in a year in history and an amount of money during that year. Once a user designates a specific amount of money, they press calculate and the website automatically figures in all of the years of inflation for the entered dates. For example, if a user saved $100 in 1980, it would have the same buying power as $275.08 in 2012. This provides users with an exceptionally accurate depiction of inflation rates. The URL is http://www.bls.gov/data/inflation_calculator.htm.

13. Performance-enhancing drugs have been prevalent in a variety of sports. Both football and baseball have had a significant number of occurrences of usage. There was a lot of media attention and publicity regarding these two sports and many of the players in them. The type of performance-enhancing drug in this book was not specified with a name or explicit definition because the goal was to look at the analytics of the Prisoner's Dilemma through the lens of this example. The actual substances used in the examples are somewhat irrelevant to explain the theory.

www.ingramcontent.com/pod-product-compliance
Lightning Source LLC
Chambersburg PA
CBHW060558200326
41521CB00007B/604